RAISED BED GARDENING FOR BEGINNERS

RAISED BED GARDENING FOR BEGINNERS 1

Introduction 4

What are raised beds? 12

Step by step instructions to Grow Well in Small Spaces .15

How do you build a raised garden bed? 28

Planting tips...29

Chapter One 37

A Beginner's Guide To Making And Sustaining Your Own Raised Bed Garden 37

Chapter Two 45

Why People Should Choose Raised Bed Gardening.......45

7 Reasons Why You Need A Raised Garden Bed (And How To Create One) 45

• how to build a raised garden bed 47

Chapter Three...53

Building Your Raised Bad Gardening 53

Useful points of raised bed cultivating 74

Why should i build a raised garden bed?.........................76

Soil for raised garden beds.................................81

Chapter Four 85

Planning Your Gardening 85

30 Raised Garden Beds Plans & Ideas You Can Build In A Day 85

Chapter Five 116

What To Grow And What Not To Grow In Your Raised Beds 116

Chapter Six 120

Basics: Gardening In Raised Beds Greenhouse........... 120

Chapter Seven 131

Planting And Maintaining Crops In Raised Bed Gardens
.... 131

5 Tips For Improving Your Raised Bed Garden Soil 131

Chapter Eight 135

Materials For Raised Garden Beds 135

Chapter Nine 143

The Best Soil Combination For Raised Garden Boxes . 143

Chapter Ten 148

Proven Tips To Help You Grow Vegetable, Herbs, And
Flowers In Your New Raised Bed 148

Five quick steps to grow fresh herbs at home step 157

Starting a flower garden 161

The most natural flowers for beginners..................... 162

Introduction

If you're looking for a more straightforward way to garden, raised bed gardening can just be your new best friend. With this method, you can grow fruit and vegetable ointments, flower wraps, and endless bunches of herbs with minimal effort. It's straightforward to garden in raised beds! To help us share the joys of this super-simple method of growing, we have teamed up with gardener's supply company, a vermont-based, employee-owned company that manufactures beautiful raised planter boxes and lots of other tools to make gardening fun and easy.

Before talking about how utilizing raised beds can end up being gainful for you, it is important to initially comprehend the benefits of the raised bed. In such manner it is very evident that such beds are adaptable and furthermore effortlessly utilized and offer various advantages that the regular nursery bed can't offer. For instance, a raised nursery bed permits you to keep close command over how you blend soil so you can develop plants with soils that suit their development to get the best outcomes.

Raising the bed by as much as eight crawls over the ground level likewise guarantees better waste. When utilizing raised bed packs there you won't need to step into the raised bed when doing plant support just as having the option to develop more vegetables because of the root room that is currently accessible to the plants.

For anybody that needs to plant utilizing a layered raised bed there is have to do some arranging great ahead of timo. It likewise helps and when you will set aside the effort to make sense of appropriate arrangement for the raised blossom garden bed to make a decent plan just as get great light before doing whatever else. You should make a sketch of your nursery and set in zones put in a safe spot for the yard just as differentiate where you expect putting walkways.

With the assistance of drafting paper and by utilizing diverse shaded pencils you can conceptualize your nursery and set out highlights in your scene, for example, walkways, turf and trees and the sky is the limit from there; each can be set apart in an exceptional shading. What's more, at that point after you have utilized your representations and structures and can purchase or fabricate your raised beds and spot them in their appropriate spot as indicated by your arrangement. You at that point blend your dirt and fill the beds right to the top since they will settle after some time. In the event that you wish to keep away from future issues, for example, illness influencing your plants you ought to pick new soil; else you can utilize soil that you can delve up in your nursery. To set aside cash, you can use about a fourth of the dirt that is acquired by uncovering the nursery and the rest can be new soil.

It is additionally essential to figure out how to utilize soil viably. And when you are not familiar with treating the soil, you ought to be as it is an attempted and tried formula that will assist you with capitalizing on the dirt in the most ideal way.

You can keep sicknesses from decimating your plants by adding extra insurance to the top just as base of your raised bed. Actually, covering the base with chicken wire is a smart thought and when you need to get creatures far from your plants. Flying creature netting on the raised bed can be utilized to keep winged animals from assaulting your products of the soil. What's more, remember to put a weed boundary between the ground and the dirt for the raised planting bed.

Mulching the raised bed can likewise help keep weeds under control and the utilization of natural mulches is absolutely the most ideal approach. If your plants become influenced by soil borne illness you should change the dirt and afterward proceed with your cultivating. This is simpler in a raised bed unit as the dirt is contained in one territory.

You should water the raised bed frequently enough that the plants are developing and the dirt is damp with no standing water in any space between lines. You ought to anyway abstain from watering your plants with a hose as this can cause the plants to turn out to be too wet which can pull in organism just as different sicknesses.

When you begin you will see that it is so natural to plant and keep up your nurseries in raised beds. It simply doesn't get a lot simpler than this.

Find raised nursery beds that are immaculate to grow a herb or vegetable nursery or bloom beds. You can likewise get natural raised beds so you can develop naturally and when you pick.

Gardening in raised beds is essentially a hybrid gardening technique. It's half a container gardening and half a bed gardening. Traditional raised beds lack a bottom and are relatively broad in size, while containers have a foundation to hold the soil and are much smaller than a raised bed. Elevated raised bed planting blends the best of the two worlds.

With this process, the soil is completely enclosed, and the growing area is vast. Then, to place the proverbial icing on the cake, raised bed gardening gives the gardener a real leg-up by raising the planting area to a working height.

There are many advantages of gardening in raised beds. Apart from the obvious benefit of never having to lean over or kneel to plant or pick your peppers and pansies, planting in an elevated planter box means that you can enjoy the following:

• no weeds (take that, bittercress!)

• no soil-dwelling pests to nibble plant roots

• no soil-borne fungal diseases to deal with

 • no rabbits and groundhogs chewing on your lettuce

• no need to set up a water sprinkler or drip device

• no issues with water-logged clay soil or fast-draining sandy soil

• no need to leave the deck or the patio for harvesting

 • no backaches, creaking knees

Selecting raised planter boxes/elevated raised beds

When shopping for an elevated raised bed, here are a few traits to keep in mind.

1. First and foremost, look for a planter that has drainage and is made of materials that will last for several years. The beautiful raised bed of gardener's supply company shown above and below, for example, is made of naturally rotating

cedar boards with robust, rust-proof aluminium legs. It can survive several seasons without any problems, and the legs can accommodate hundreds of pounds of soil and plant material. They also give different colour options to the planter box.

2. Make sure that your elevated planter box is an excellent place to grow food. If you are preparing to grow edibles, it should be free of pesticides, toxic paints and stains, and chemically treated trees.

. First, consider the scale of the planter. Elevated raised bed gardening ensures that the height of the bed would limit the roots of your plants. Make sure the raised planter you select is deep enough to handle root crops, such as carrots and parsnips, and offers plenty of space for the roots of larger plants, such as tomatoes, eggplants, sunflowers, and others. The size of the planter box in this article is 92" long, 24" full and 10" deep — perfect for a broad range of flowers, fruits, vegetables and herbs! If that's too long for your room, gardener's supply company also has a four-foot-long bunk bed available.

3. The total height of your raised bed garden is also significant. When it's too big, you'll get tired of reaching up, but if it's not far enough, you'll have a slight natural bend in

your back in the short order of the chiropractor.

4. Eventually, it is necessary to recognize the maintenance needs of the planter. Elevated raised bed gardening is intended to make your life simpler, not to complicate it. Skip planter boxes that need painting or staining on an annual basis or those that rust, warp or become brittle with excessive exposure to sunlight.

5. Placing your raised garden planter once you've selected the raised bed that's perfect for you, it's time to put it in place. Such farmers are massive when they are filled to the brim with dirt, so don't fill the planter box until you're comfortable with its location.

Many fruits and vegetables need at least 6 to 8 hours of full sun. Gardeners intending to grow edibles while raised bed gardening need to put the planters in full sun. If you are rising sun-loving annuals, the rule is the same. But for those who enjoy the shade, a right spot in the shade or part of the shadow will do just fine.

Also, make sure that your elevated planter box is close to a spigot or rain barrel to allow a snap of watering. Lugging watering cans to a remote place every day can be a real drag. Holding your garden near the kitchen door is a bonus, too!

Filling your raised planter box as with in-ground growing, the secret to edible raised bed gardening is in the soil. Although most elevated planter boxes are durable, they are not designed to carry thick, clay-based garden soil. Instead, they are built to be filled with a mixture of high-quality potting soil and compost. Mix 2/3 potting soil with 1/3 compost, throw in a few handfuls of organic granular fertilizer, and you'll be ready to grow! (unless, of course, you grow cacti or succulents in your raised planter; in that case, apply coarse builder sand to the mix instead of compost.) How to build for raised bed gardening for it comes to growing in raised planters, the options are limitless! There are so many plants that are going to do wonderfully in such a setting.

• plant an elevated bed full of lightweight vegetable varieties, including 'tumbling tom' tomatoes, 'fairy tale' aubergines, 'mohawk patio' peppers and 'thumbelina' carrots.

• or what about creating a green paradise? 'Spicy globe' basil, creeping thyme, lemongrass, rosemary and parsley would be beautiful.

• small-scale berry plants, such as 'strawberry shortcake' red raspberries, 'top hat' blueberries and strawberries, are beautiful and productive in a raised bed.

• the flowers are just another lovely choice. Most annuals do very well in raised planters, just be sure to add a few trailing varieties to spill over the edge of the garden.

• fairy gardens and miniature plants are another unique choices, mainly because they will be at eye level for curious little hands and eyes.

• you can also grow miniature flowering shrubs and small evergreens while planting in a raised bed. Doing so is going to make a perfect privacy screen between the surrounding balconies, patios and porches.

Any gardener knows that getting the right soil will make a difference in achieving excellent results in the garden. Sadly, not every yard is blessed with fertile, high-quality soil. Growing bed gardening is the ideal solution. You can monitor your soil by using raised beds,

What are raised beds?

The raised bed is essentially a full, over-ground planter, with walls varying from 6-24 inches high. Generally, these beds are enclosed in some kind of frame, usually made of wood, concrete or stone. Once the bed housing has been installed, it is filled with soil-forming an ugly, but a practical planter. If the area where the bed is installed has low soil quality, it can be used outside the soil.

Growing beds can be used to build just about everything. They make excellent vegetable planters, can be a lovely way to show off vegetables, and are the best choice for shrubs, fruits and herbs. When properly built, raised beds can be a beautiful way to establish distinct planting areas in the garden.

What are the cons of elevated beds?

There are many advantages to making this kind of garden bed. One of the significant benefits is that you can choose which type of soil to fill a planter with, which gives you full control over soil quality and nutrition. It can be a great help if your backyard soil is made up of sand or hard clay. Raised beds often prolong the growing season as they warm up much earlier in the spring. This will require earlier planting and cultivation in the garden. They foster good soil drainage and help you achieve the perfect water balance for each of your plants.

Another great advantage of the raised garden bed is the ease of entry. Most gardeners carefully design the width of their beds (usually no more than 4 feet) to ensure that the whole planting area is accessible from the sides. This will make gardening easier for those who have a hard time kneeling to plant and weed their garden. The raised beds, correctly built, can also be used in wheelchairs. The high concept also stops you from compacting the soil and crushing plants.

What are the cons of raised beds?

Raised beds are a convenient gardening choice, but they're not without their downfalls. One downside is that they usually have to be grown by hand. Garden tillers are almost impossible to use in a raised bed. Nonetheless, if you continue to change the soil with high-quality compost, the land will remain viable with no need for digging. Another con is the initial time and cost needed to build these beds. If you want to build foundations on your own or use a pre-made kit, it can be expensive and will take time to set up and install properly.

Placing your beds

Placing your beds is very important and will rely on what you want to expand. For example, tomatoes need at least 8 hours of direct sunlight, while shade-loving plants prefer minimal sunlight. Determine what you're going to plant and then find a place that will provide perfect light and growing conditions. Consider also its ease of access from your house, the location of your water source, and proximity to pests such as deer and rabbits.

The area will also have to be correctly prepared before planting can begin. One of the first things you want to do is clear any weeds and foliage from the field. It can be done by manual digging to clear the sod to get to the bare soil. Covering the area with black plastic sheeting or a thick layer of mulch for several months can make the work much more manageable. If you are constructing a full raised bed (12 inches or more), you can leave the grass in place, put some paper or paper bags down to smother the grass, and simply add the soil to the top. Within a few months, the document would disintegrate. If burrowing animals like moles plague your yard, you may want to consider installing chicken wire in the bottom of your bed — but whatever you do, make sure that earthworms can get into your beds to keep the soil safe.

Step by step instructions to Grow Well in Small Spaces

Raised beds was never considered as one of the vegetable planting tips of the day. All things considered, times have changes, and raised beds are perceived for their numerous points of interest. We should all consider raised beds as one of the extraordinary vegetable cultivating tips, regardless of whether we garden outside or practice nursery planting.

A raised bed nursery can be utilized for yards that have poor soil and seepage issues. The possibility of a raised bed is to work over the ground, where you don't need to fight against poor soil and terrible waste. You additionally have complete command over the dirt surface, substance and seepage.

A raised bed garden is a nursery that is over the ground and contained in a zone with high sides. The plant specialist strolls between the beds and it is a sorted out approach to cultivate. It tends to be any profundity you pick and can be utilized for all intents and purposes anything you wish to plant. Herbs developed in raised beds have a preferred position over in the ground developing for a couple of reasons.

Review that corrosive soils contain a pH estimation underneath the typical 6.5-7.5 territory. Contingent upon which region of the nation you live in, the odds are acceptable that at any rate a part of your arranged nursery may contain acidic soils.

Obviously, there are some more, yet that will serve to give you a case of a few. Additionally recollect that corrosive soils will in general hold dampness, so you may need to work in a decent measure of natural issue to help waste.

In the event that you have verified that your dirt is exceptionally antacid, and you truly need to plant those azaleas or those rhododendrons, about the main way you will get victories in your nursery region is and when you make them an uncommon bed, called a raised bed. Commonly, this structure is made from any number of woods, for example, posts, railroad ties or stacked 2x4's. Individuals additionally make raised beds out of block and droop stones, however to minimize expenses, wood is your most logical option.

Cultivating in raised beds has been drilled in the United States since the provincial days. It made a major rebound during the 60's, and afterward blurred once more, however the 21st century has seen a developing resurgence of prevalence among home vegetable producers. In parts of the world with more prominent populace densities or less tillable land, yard cultivating is still intensely rehearsed.

"Raised" implies that the dirt level in the bed is higher than encompassing soil, and "bed" infers a size little enough to work without really venturing onto the region utilized. A raised bed ought to be close to 4 feet wide, while length can be whatever suits the site or individual nursery worker's needs. More extensive beds can be partitioned into segments open from pavers, venturing stones or boards whenever wanted.

There are a few distinct explanations behind making a raised bed, a significant number of them useful, others progressively tasteful in nature. The absolute most normal reasons are:

More significant returns: A raised bed gives more creation per square foot of nursery. In a conventional home nursery, great administration may yield about 0.6 pounds of vegetables per square foot while a raised bed may twofold that sum. What's more, raised beds don't require the standard space between columns, in light of the fact that no strolling is done in the bed to develop or gather.

Improved Soil Conditions: Typically, soil compaction decreases many harvest yields by up to 50 percent. Water, air and roots all experience issues traveling through soil compacted by tractors, tillers or human feet, yet plant specialists can keep away from the issue by making beds sufficiently tight to work from the sides. Soil natural issue substance can be expanded incredibly without getting stalled.

Brought beds likewise help up in issue soil circumstances where planters must arrangement with low spots unsuited for ordinary nurseries due to disintegration from overflow. Raised beds, utilizing outlines as an establishment, stay away from this issue and soil causticity can be kept up in the

5.8 to 6.8-pH extend, which is ideal for most vegetables.

Simpler Working Conditions: The most significant advantage of cultivating with raised beds is the expanded simplicity of planting and reaping. Numerous individuals abstain from working conventional gardens in stormy climate to maintain a strategic distance from compaction and sloppy feet. Since raised beds are intended to abstain from stomping on, nursery workers maintain a strategic distance from sloppy feet. Spaces between beds might be mulched or even cleared with stone or block.

Better Pest Control: Pest control likewise turns out to be less troublesome in raised beds. In the event that tunneling rodents are plentiful, the base of the bed can be fixed with poultry wire or equipment fabric. Setting most loved nourishments in a confined bed with a low fence can hinder hares and groundhogs from attacking your vegetable nursery. The tight elements of raised beds make it simpler to spread feathered creature netting suspended on edges to shield them from pecking at leaves and vegetables, and weed control with plastic sheeting is a lot simpler, as the width of the bed can be traversed by one roll.

Water Conservation: The restricted elements of beds make them perfect for water preservation. Canvas soaker hoses and dribble type water system hoses direct water to the dirt where it is required most and diminish malady issues which happen from watering with overhead sprayers or sprinklers.

Corrosive Loving Plants: It might be that your dirt is acidic and you end up adjusting to the plants and bushes you have decided for your nursery to suit corrosive cherishing plants, or you may likewise find that your dirt is about consummately adjusted in pH levels and that you don't have acidic soils. You can pick some normal plants that lean toward acidic soil, for example,

1) Rock rose

2) Azalea

3) Rhododendron

4) Witch Hazel

5) Camellia

6) Bearberry

7) Dogwood

8) Trumpet Vine

9) Wisteria

We should take a gander at the upsides of raised beds. A raised bed for vegetable cultivating will help:

Limit twisting around to plant, weed and collect. Indeed, even a raised bed of 6 inches makes planting simpler on the back. You can bow adjacent to the bed, however you don't need to twist around to collect ground level vegetables since they are raised higher for your benefit.

Warm the dirt faster in the spring. The sides of raised beds are presented to spring and summer warmth, so the dirt above evaluation (in the raised bed) gets warm speedier and remains warm all through the developing season. Soil temperature is indispensable for development, so a raised bed makes a pleasant showing of normally supporting this plant need.

Characterize and arrange planting zones. A raised bed offers "compartments" to develop in, in this manner making it simpler to appoint garden space to assortments. It likewise characterizes garden walkways.

Limit ill-disposed contact between plants. Raised beds are regularly isolated by ways, and these stomped on pathways are not helpful for plant roots, in this way permitting us to keep one plant enemy in nearness to another. And when tall beds are utilized, for example, 55 gallon drums, foes can be planted adjoining each another as there is 3 feet of soil for roots to enter before they interact with different roots.

Give further soil to plants. A decent way to deal with raising vegetables is to give however much soil as could reasonably be expected for roots to enter, spread out and ingest supplements. Raised beds give additional dirt above evaluation, so plants have significantly more soil to flourish in.

Consider better seepage. By their very nature, a raised bed is definitely not a low territory where water can collect. Seepage is advanced as raised beds are higher than wherever water would normally settle.

There you have it. Raised beds offer numerous advantages,

and they can be produced using a wide scope of materials. The materials you select ought to be founded on weight, cost and accommodation. What's more, obviously, your energy for development.

"Raised" implies that the dirt level in the bed is higher than encompassing soil, and "bed" suggests a size little enough to work without really venturing onto the territory utilized. Regularly, this structure is made from any number of woods, for example, posts, railroad ties or stacked 2x4's. Individuals likewise make raised beds out of block and droop stones, however to minimize expenses, wood is your most solid option. There are a few distinct purposes behind making a raised bed, a significant number of them down to earth, others increasingly tasteful in nature.

There are the same number of approaches to structure a nursery as there are various sorts of nurseries themselves. One type of planting that is turning out to be progressively well known is raised bed cultivating. Raised bed cultivating comprises of planting in raised beds of soil, regardless of whether in enormous grower boxes, or much greater regions you build yourself. Raised bed planting has numerous important points, and a couple of hindrances also. A survey of the advantages and disadvantages can be useful in choosing if this sort of planting is for you.

Geniuses:

1. And when you have poor soil, raised bed gardens permit you to set up your own rich blend of soil over the ground for developing your plants.

2. Your planting regions will be simpler to get to in light of the fact that you won't need to twist around so much, accordingly lessening exhaustion and injury to the knees and back.

3. Raised beds are additionally perfect for older or incapacitated plant specialists who can't reach to the cold earth, and they can be developed at practically any stature to address the nursery worker's issues

4. Plants are anything but difficult to keep sorted out. For instance, you can plant tomatoes in a single raised segment and peppers in another.

5. Dead leaves and other nursery flotsam and jetsam will be restricted to their own region, helping you keep up a tidier look in your yard.

6. You can get ready unique beds of soil custom fitted to different plants. For instance, plants that need a profoundly acidic soil can be gathered in one territory, and you can set up the dirt to the correct pH explicitly for their necessities.

7. In substantial downpours, there is less possibility of soil disintegration.

8. Hares, moles, and other nursery bugs are more averse to have the option to get to your plants.

9. Raised bed gardens are perfect for longer established yields, for example, carrots that need a few creeps to a foot of good quality soil.

10. Raised bed cultivating is an extraordinary choice in the event that you have next to no space. Raised planting

territories can even be developed on a little deck or porch zone for growing an assortment of herbs, vegetables, or blossoms.

Cons:

1. Any working will most likely must be finished by hand. It's hard to utilize tractors or revolving tillers in raised planting regions.

2. The underlying in advance expense of developing raised bed gardens is more costly than basically working a conventional nursery into your dirt. Nonetheless, units can be bought online that make the development procedure quicker and simpler.

3. The edges or outskirts of the planting territories must be all around strengthened during the underlying development, or they may start to separate after some time, making and continuous upkeep issue.

4. And when you live in a dry atmosphere, raised beds will dry out quicker and require increasingly visit watering. Then again, and when you live in an extremely soggy atmosphere, your plants will be less powerless to root decay from over watering.

5. Raised planting territories are not reasonable to vining or rambling plants, for example, pumpkins, squash, watermelons, or different climbing plants, for example, morning greatness, clematis, or trumpet vine.

6. The materials utilized for developing raised bed nurseries ought to be deliberately thought of. Treated wood or railroad ties absorbed creosote ought not be utilized. These synthetic substances will spill out into the dirt after some time, harming and killing your plants.

Placing in raised beds can be a major interest in time and cash, however it will likewise take care of you in better plants, all the more cultivating room, and simpler access to your planting regions. A cautious assessment of the considerable number of advantages and disadvantages will assist you with settling on the correct choice for you and your yard. Whatever your choice, cautious arranging is consistently the way to victories in the nursery.

How do you build a raised garden bed?

Creating a raised garden bed is a relatively straightforward process if you have the right equipment and a plan in place before you get started. You can use raised bed kits from garden supply centres, or you can build your own from scratch. The first thing you want to do is choose the materials you're going to use to create your bed. You can use almost everything from wood to concrete to stone and even materials found around your house. When selecting your products, it is essential to consider what chemicals can be leached into the soil. Non-toxic materials are particularly important when growing vegetables or other edible plants since any substances in the soil can be produced.

When you have decided which materials to use, you may start the construction process. Take the time to make your frame stable and safe, as it will help to last and reduce soil erosion. When the structure has been built, it should be lined with dirt. This is an excellent opportunity for you to develop a soil mix that will help your plants flourish, so choose a soil that is suitable for the type of plant you are planning to grow. Mixing sand in your soil will enhance your drainage, and the use of organic matter such as peat moss or compost will help to retain optimum soil moisture levels.

Planting tips

Once your beds have been built, they are ready for planting. You can plant several different fruits, vegetables and floral decorations in the same field, or you can split various kinds of plants.

• think about plant placement: tall plants should be placed in the centre of your bed or on one side so that they do not obstruct access to other plants or produce unnecessary shades.

• pay attention to planting guidelines: raised beds should be ready for spring planting earlier than unraised beds. Follow the unique planting guidelines for every plant you select from. Plant too first and your plants will freeze, but plant too late in the season and you will not have enough time to grow until the season is over ultimately.

• fertilizer is essential: the proper fertilization of your plants will help your plants develop. While applying fertilizer, aim to spread around the base of the plant to prevent contact with the leaves of the plant.

1.built-in raised beds

Raised bed planting involves growing plants in beds that are higher than the surface. Most commonly, you can do this with some kind of enclosure or frame made of wood, stone, or even hay bales or recycled material like old dressers.

Growing beds can be as modest or imaginative as you want. A raised bed planter can be a permanent fixture for perennial plants to grow in and mature. The initial cost of setting up your raised bed will depend on how intricate you make it, but once in place, the raised beds are no more costly to maintain than the conventional gardens. They're providing a lot of benefits.

When you make a raised bed instead of going in-ground, you can put it where the sun or shade is better suited to the plants you want to grow. You will also avoid the decimation of your plants by tunnelling pests. Plants can be safer and more efficient in a raised bed because you can monitor soil quality and water drainage. When you create the sides large enough to make a bench, you can even sit down and have a garden, which makes it easier for those with back problems to tend the plants.

2. Sheet metal raised beds

Another great benefit of raised bed gardens is that they sit just above the underground frost line, so the soil warms up more quickly in the spring, so you can start planting more easily. Metal must ensure that the ambient heat from the sun is retained in the soil. Sheet metal is more natural to mould. This is also a perfect way to provide the heat required to grow mediterranean plants such as sage and lavender.

3. Square foot raised beds

Square foot gardening requires dividing the growing area into small rectangular sections, usually one foot per piece. The goal is to grow an intensively planted vegetable garden or a highly successful kitchen garden.

Use a raised bed for growing vegetables; you can monitor the consistency of the soil and prevent it from being compacted. Vegetable roots can grow unimpeded. The beds don't have to be very far off the ground to get the advantages of sleeping in a raised bed. There should be plenty of 6 to 8 inches.

These vegetable beds are enough to increase the drainage of water. This garden uses the mel bartholomew square fool gardening technique to make the layout simpler and the harvesting amp.

3. Herb spiral

Spiral gardens, like the mill creek gardens herb garden, are a common permaculture technique. They can increase the amount of available planting area without taking up more ground space in your garden. You can quickly build them out of stone, brick, wood, or just dig up the dirt. The odd shape and swirl of plants make your garden an eye-catching important point. Herbs are the plants of choice in this shot, but you can grow anything with a spiral design.

5. Hoop house raised bed

With a bit of pre-planning, you can build a multi-season vegetable garden. Raised beds give you more room to manage growing conditions in your yard and make it harder for animals to get to your vegetables.

If you build a hoop house on top of a raised bed, you can be prepared for any season, manage the freeze, and give yourself a spring start.

6. Raised bed border

Raised beds are a perfect choice for yards with steep slopes. By building up the mattresses in their lowest parts, like these stone beds, you can create the impression of a level garden. Design your beds large enough so that you can still have a layered flower garden with a border of shrubs encircling the back of the garden and plenty of space for perennials that will give you colours, textures, and edge-soft drapes.

7. Trough gardens beautiful faux

Creations illustrate one of the simplest ways to build raised bed gardens by using animal feed troughs. There is no assembly needed, but be sure to drill some of the drainage holes in the bottom before you add the soil. The metal gives the garden an industrial look and heats the land in the spring. Depending on what you want to grow, the plants can need some extra water during the hottest part of the summer.

8. Custom-designed raised beds

The raised bed gardens can fit just about any space. With a little imagination, you can create a whole garden sitting area. This multi-level raised bed incorporated the clear straight lines of peter donegan landscaping. It comes with a potting shed and a lamppost. Attach a bench part, like the one at the end of the front room, and you've got an outdoor dining area. As the plants and the woods fill up, this garden will have a perfect, rustic look.

9. Raised bed arbor

The use of a trellis or arbour with a raised bed makes it much easier to grow vegetables and keep them healthier than if they were spread out on the grass. Vertical gardening enables you to become more plants without taking up more space.

This example of family food gardens shows that whether you grow flowering vines or spreading vegetables, this garden teepee trellis provides a living tree that gives the grapes plenty of access to sunlight without shading the plants in the raised beds below. Your concept can be as easy as making an a-frame by leaning two bamboo poles together, tie them together, and extending the garden net around.

10. Architectural

Architecture gardens in small spaces can always feel cluttered and unfinished. At the other side, the raised beds that line this pathway garden look like it was well thought out. You can also schedule your planting to give you four seasons of visual interest, as shown, in this small garden. Shape beds in every one

The design of bricks, pavements, or composite flooring material. Not only do they define the yard, but they also make the garden appear more substantial by breaking up the view and offering an extra seating area in the shady part of the garden.

11. Colourful concrete block garden

There are many ways to create raised beds with recycled materials. Concrete blocks are one of the most common ones. This gardener at home built inspired took it one step further and decorated their block garden with a little colourful paint. Remember that some of the older cinder blocks can contain fly ash, which is the "cinders" leftover from burning coal. Whether this is safe to use among edible plants is still under consideration. If you get new blocks made of concrete, you can avoid the ash problem. The modern blocks are much more massive than the older cinder blocks but are safe to use for a vegetable garden. Be careful, though — the concrete blocks of leech lime. Lime can increase the ph of the soil. To be healthy, use plants that thrive in alkaline soil

12. Tiered low bed

Floor beds have very few drawbacks. This multi-tiered elevated bed from home stratosphère looks like a pagoda or a fountain. When the flowers grow out, you may not even see a beautiful wooden frame supporting them. It looks pretty good all year long. You can also decorate it with festive greens and lights during the holidays and make it look like a christmas tree 13. Garage doors re-purposed as a garden look in your storage area or check out some of the shelter shops for things lying around that would make them appealing, easy-to-assemble raised beds. The gardener at life at the cottage planned her kitchen garden with some vinyl garage door panels attached to resin reinforced vinyl fence posts and finishes. This raised bed looks stylish, has low maintenance, does not need waterproofing or painting, and will last longer than most wood products.

14. Sunken raised bed

Rather than just terracing the entire area of the sloping yard, you might create an eye-level garden. Maria michelle photographed this seating area on the hillside. A stone patio and retaining walls create an inviting garden path and a seating area surrounded by raised beds. This scene involved a lot of soil removal and stonework, but it would last for years to come.

. 15. Milk crate garden

Drop the milk crates and make your raised bed portable. This milk crate raised bed is comfortable to set up and can be adjusted to any shape you want. If you need your plants closer to your kitchen, or you want to position them in a shadier spot, just pick up the crate and go. Such tanks also have drainage holes in them. So when you need to adjust the soil, you can only raise the box so pour the contents of the compost pile and continue again.

Chapter One

A Beginner's Guide To Making And Sustaining Your Own Raised Bed Garden

Growing your vegetables is fun and satisfying. All you need is some good soil and a few plants to get started. But to be a genuinely useful vegetable gardener—and do it organically—you'll need to realize what it takes to keep your plants healthy and vigorous. Those are the rules.

"feed the soil" is like a mantra for organic gardeners, and with good reason. Indeed, in modern chemical agriculture, crop plants are correctly "fed" using synthetic fertilizers.

When taken to extremes, this kind of chemical force-feeding that slowly impoverish the soil. And transform it from a vibrant entity teeming with microorganisms insects and other life forms, into an inert growing medium which exists mainly to anchor the roots of plants, and which provides little to no nutrition in its own right.

Although various fertilizers and mineral nutrients (agricultural lime, rock phosphate, green sand, etc.) Can be applied regularly to the organic garden, organic matter is by far the most valuable material for creating and preserving a safe, well-balanced soil. Organic matter may be applied to the land in some ways, such as compost, shredded leaves, animal manures or crops.

Organic matter increases the fertility, structure and tilth of soils of all kinds. In particular, organic matter is a continuous source of nitrogen and other nutrients that plants need to grow. It also provides a rich source of food for soil microbes. When soil organisms conduct decay and decomposition processes, these nutrients are made available to plants. Learn all about creating good soil.

Make effective use of space

 The location of your garden (the amount of sunlight it receives, proximity to the water supply, and protection from frost and wind) is essential. However, just as crucial to growing vegetables is making the most of your garden area.

A lot of people dream of having a massive vegetable garden, a sprawling site that's going to be large enough to grow everything they want, including space-hungry crops such as corn, dried beans, pumpkins and winter squash, melons, cucumbers and melons. If you have space and, more importantly, the time and energy you need to grow a large garden well, go for it. Yet vegetable gardens that allow proper use of growing space are much easier to look after, whether you're talking about a few containers on the patio or a 50-by-100-foot plot in the backyard. Rising beds are the right choice for beginners, as they make the garden more manageable.

Get rid of your rows

The first way to maximize space in the garden is to move from conventional rows of planting to 3or 4-foot-wide raised beds. Single rows of crops, though they may be active on farms that use large machines for planting, growing and harvesting, are often not the best way to go in the backyard garden. In a home-sized garden, the fewer rows you've got, the fewer paths between rows you'll need, and the more square footage you'll have for growing crops.

When you're already growing the amount of food you want in your current row garden, you'll be able to reduce the size of the garden by converting to raised beds or open beds. By removing this existing garden area, you can plant green manure crops on the part of the garden that does not currently grow vegetables and rotates growing areas more easily from year to year. Or you might find that you now have room to plant new crops — rhubarb, asparagus, berries, or cut flowers — in the newly available space.

Many good reasons to switch from rows to an intensive gardening system: less energy. If vegetables are planted intensively, they shade and cool the soil below and need less watering, less weeding, less mulching — in other words, less drudgery for the gardener.

Less compaction of the soil. The more you have access between rows or fields, the more you and others can compress the ground by walking in them. By increasing the width of the growing beds and reducing the number of paths, you will have more growing areas that you will not walk on, and this unpaved soil will be more moist and ideal for the roots of the plants.

Grow up, not out

Compared to intensive planting, trellising is the most effective way to use space in the yard. Those who have tiny gardens will want to grow as many crops as possible on vertical supports, and gardeners who have a lot of space will also need to provide physical support to some of their vegetables, such as peas and pomegranate varieties. Other plants that are usually roasted include vineyard varieties, such as cucumbers and tomatoes.

The fence around your garden could well be double-duty as a trellis, as long as the crops grown on the wall can be rotated in different years. Other kinds of vegetable supports are usually made of either wood or metal. Nevertheless, no matter what design or materials you use, make sure to have

your trellis in place well before the plants need support—
preferably even before you plant the seed. With some
vegetables, such as tomatoes or melons, you may also need
to gently tie the plants to the support or tie them through the
trellis as they grow.

Keeping crops moving

Crop rotation within the vegetable garden means planting
the same crop at the same place just once every three
years. This strategy ensures that the same vegetable garden
does not deplete the same nutrients year after year. It can
also help to foil any insect pests or disease pathogens that
can be lingering in the soil after harvesting.

To use a three-year crop rotation method, make a garden
plan on paper for every growing season, showing the
position of all crops. If like most people, you're growing a lot
of different vegetables, these garden plans are invaluable,
since it can be hard to remember exactly what you've been
building since just last season, less than two years ago.
Saving garden plans for the past two or three years means
you don't have to rely on memory alone.

Continuous harvest

Planting a crop in succession is just another way to optimize
the growing area in the greenhouse. Far too often, however,

gardeners will prepare their seedbeds and plant or transplant now their crops for only one or two days in the spring, usually after the last frost date for their area.

Although there's nothing wrong with planting a garden this way, wouldn't it be easier to plant a few seeds or transplants at a time, during the whole growing season, than to face the arduous task of "get in the field" all at once?

After all, it's almost always more comfortable to work the further you split it. Intend to plant something fresh in the garden nearly every week of the season, from the first cold-hardy greens and peas in late winter or early spring, to sun-loving transplants such as tomatoes, peppers and eggplant once the weather is dry and humid.

Then continue again, sowing frost-hardy crops from mid-summer to mid-summer, depending on your climate. Hold the beds clean as you harvest the crops to make room for the new vegetables that will take their place. You can also plant crops that overgrow (radish) alongside other veggies that need a long season (carrots or parsnips) and sow their seeds together. This makes it easier to thin the bed later, as you'll have already harvested a quick-growing crop and long-season vegetables that remain some much-needed elbow space.

Another advantage of succession planting, of course, is that the harvest season lasts longer with any crop. It ensures that instead of being covered in snap beans or summer squash when your plants grow all at once, you can stagger plantings to ensure a consistent but more manageable supply of fresh vegetables.

Print your plans

When you are using our kitchen garden planner, you can print your plans, make notes and save them for future seasons.

Last but not least, we end up where we started — with the realization that, while vegetable gardening can be satisfying even for beginners, there is an art to do it well. There is also a range of useful knowledge and advice from other gardeners at your fingertips. Yet one of the most effective ways to improve your garden from year to year is to pay careful attention to how plants grow and to record your achievements and shortcomings in a garden notebook or journal.

Much like drawing a garden plan each year helps you remember where things were developing, taking notes will help you avoid making the same mistakes again, or make sure that your good results can be repeated in future years. For example, write down all the names of the different types of vegetables and compare them from year to year, so you'll know which ones you've done well in your garden.

A lot of people keep a book in their car to record when they change their oil and do other daily maintenance. In the same way, get used to jotting it down if you add organic matter or fertilizer to the greenhouse, or when you plant or start harvesting a crop.

Over time, this kind of careful observation and record-keeping will probably tell you more about growing vegetables than any single book or authority. That's because the notes you make should be focused on your own experience and experiences, representing what works best for you in the special conditions of your garden. As with so many other activities, so is the art of vegetable gardening: practice is excellent.

Chapter Two

Why People Should Choose Raised Bed Gardening

7 Reasons Why You Need A Raised Garden Bed (And How To Create One)

Kip the open ground and move to the higher ground to plant your favourite plants. Due to the raised beds, your garden can be almost anywhere in your yard while preserving perfect soil conditions and growing conditions.

Gardeners everywhere have raised beds, and we're sure you'll love them as well. Here are seven reasons why you need a raised garden bed—we're even going to show you how to make your own! Follow our simple instructions to make your backyard room with a 3x5-foot raised bed.

1. **Simple garden maintenance**

    Having a raised bed makes it easier to keep your plants going. There's less leaning over the foundations that are elevated off the ground. Create them with large borders, and you may even be able to sit while you're working.

2. Better soil drainage

The raised beds allow the soil to drain better. Loamy soil (or loose, crumbly soil) means better-drained earth. And because the land in the raised bed is never stepped on, it is uncompacted so that it usually drains better than flatbeds.

3.extended growing

Season as the garden bed is higher; the soil appears to get warmer in the spring. Plant your seeds earlier in the spring so that you can enjoy your garden for a more extended season.

4.keeps grass from spreading

It's harder for turf to spread to raised beds. Once you build a raised bed, mow the site to keep the grass as short as possible.

5. Protect plants from animals

Building a raised bed reduces foot traffic in your yard. Access from both sides makes it, so you don't have to place a foot in your garden to weed, plant, or drink. These often have a small measure of defence against critters such as moles and voles.

6. Less space between rows equals more space you can fill

with plants. Raised beds are well suited for small vegetable crops and flowers.

7. Soil health management

Raised beds provide an ideal growing medium from scratch for those that have no soil or are compacted, rocky or deteriorated. If you're building a garden bed, you can also avoid too-wet or too-dry dirt by filling yours with rich loam.

10 excellent reasons for using raised beds in your garden

The raised bed is, by nature, a garden bed that is set up instead of down, in a position to overcome all sorts of gardening challenges. You may build raised beds only by heaping soil into a mound, or by using boxes to enclose and hold garden soil. Garden boxes are also synonymous with raised beds, as some retaining wall or material needs almost always to be used to protect the stability of the mattress over time.

• how to build a raised garden bed

• where to buy raised garden beds and raised bed components as you identify them, raised garden beds to give benefits to all types of gardeners. Here are just 10 of the many explanations for using raised beds:

1. **Less tilling is better for the soil**

A raised bed is just a way to set up the soil for the most natural possible gardening—the kind of 'no effort.' instead of tilling the soil from year to year to add fertilizer and alter, gardeners typically keep their raised beds by merely adding materials to the surface.

Compost, mulches, manures and other soil conditioners may all be added directly to the top few inches of the soil without the need for backbreaking. And the earth will do its own tilling, as the worms and roots work their way through. Although daily human-handed tilling tends to deplete the soil structure, doing nothing builds up the organic portion of your soil over time.

2. Your back is going to thank you.

It's incredible how much back and knee strain can happen just by weeding a garden, particularly a big one, and this can take a severe toll over time. A raised bed, particularly those at least 12″ tall, can relieve chronic back pain and joint pain. Only young people who are interested in farming as a career choice should consider the possible harm to the back that organic farming can do by hand weeding. Find elevated beds as a wellness benefit.

3. Raised beds look better

It may sound like mere vanity, but having better beds may have a practical function. In the city, particularly if you're trying to get away with a front yard vegetable garden, a raised bed might be a must to keep your neighbours happy. The raised beds often make the paths a little easier to maintain, since there is a clear line between the bed and the road.

4. Raised beds help keep out critters

Slugs can climb, but the high sides of the raised garden box slow them down and give them a chance to stop in their tracks. A lot of gardeners swear that slugs won't crawl over the copper flashing, which can surround your package. You may also add hardware cloth at the bottom of the box to avoid creeping critters like groundhogs from stealing root crops. And because of their height, dogs are less likely to urinate directly to your plants. When there is an issue with deer, you can connect deer fencing directly to your bed or buy a box with a built-in deer fence. This is also much simpler to attach plastic hoops to raised garden beds for bird fences, cold frames, or row covers.

5. Raising the soil means improved drainage

 In areas that are prone to floods, or in marshy yards, a raised garden bed could be the only way to provide a full growing season. The most common depth for a raised bed is 11", which is one inch below the sides of a 12" big garden box. It is ample irrigation for most crops, and it gives plants

About one foot of extra breathing space above damp conditions. In general, raised beds often tend to drain better, even in heavy rains.

• how to set up built beds on sloping, rocky ground 6. Tips for preparing the soil for your raised garden beds and planters

6. You're going to have fewer weeds and crabgrass

Tilling simply produces more pots by burying weed seeds and allowing them the perfect opportunity to spread. Successfully raised bed growers to promise to destroy all the plants that grew up in the winter by covering their beds with mulch, cardboard, or black plastic in the spring. Once it's time to start planting again, simply scrape off the dead weeds before they have a chance to get a seed. One of the most successful ways to combat crabgrass is via a raised bed. Place a weed barrier at least 10" high on the bottom of the beds to avoid the grass from infiltrating.

7. You may plant raised beds earlier in the season

 Mainly due to improved soil drainage, early planting in raised beds is possible as the soil dries out quicker in the spring and warms up faster for planting than dirt at ground level. Some gardeners often consider a large number of plants overwintered in a raised bed that shouldn't have been able to do so. Again, a lot of this has to do with the form of soil in the garden. If the soil is saturated and reinforced with compost, the temperature of the earth is better controlled than the disturbed, nutrient-poor ground.

8. Raised beds could be temporary

 Tenants who are struggling to have a garden should start a discussion with their landlord by showing them a beautiful picture of a raised bed. A tidy, tidy and well-built garden box will improve property values and be a charm instead of an eye. If the landlord still says no, a temporary garden can be installed using a portable garden box. The box is simply set to the table, the carton is put over the grass within, and the box is filled with dirt. Once you move, take the box with you, scatter the earth, and put down the grass seed again.

9. Raised beds avoid polluted soil

The urban gardeners are at higher risk of ingesting heavy metals, including lead. Many different vegetables, notably roots, tomatoes and greens, absorb heavy metals from polluted soils and can pose a real danger. Placing beds away from the road, exploring the past uses of your land, and planting thick hedges can all help, but raised beds offer a rare opportunity to put in fresh soils that have not been exposed to any contamination on the field. Toxicity is also significantly decreased by adding compost, diluting year-on-year pollution concentrations and binding of heavy metals to soil particles (just another amazing application of fertiliser!).

10. Raised beds are perfect for beginners

 Raised beds offer a simple way to start gardening by removing a lot of obstacles for beginners. We take a little more effort forward, but in other respects, we guarantee success in the first year. Attach a box, some soil, some fertilizer, some seeds, some water, and something is going to grow. "row crows" can't say the same success: sow, fertilize, sow again, crop, plant, weed... The cycle isn't as straightforward as the direction of the raised bed.

Chapter Three

Building Your Raised Bad Gardening

Raised garden beds are relatively comfortable to build, much more convenient to maintain, and offer a variety of benefits to your garden (and you)! Here's how to create a raised garden bed in your backyard, as well as some tips on how to use the right wood and soil.

Made beds are a simple way to get into the garden! Whether you buy a kit or build your own, there are a lot of good reasons to use raised bed gardening.

The raised bed vegetable nursery framework an incredible choice for developing vegetables on the grounds that, regardless of where you live, you can utilize this framework.

The raised bed vegetable nursery can be as basic or as intricate as you wish. For whatever length of time that you utilize the standards related with this sort of nursery bed then you can hope to get extraordinary outcomes with an abundance of new solid vegetables.

Developing Vegetables In Raised Beds

This sort of nursery is something like developing vegetables in holders just the 'compartment' can be so a lot bigger.

For developing vegetables, the dirt shouldn't be extremely profound as most vegetables don't have profound roots separated from the root crop vegetables that is and afterward a profundity of around 12 to 15 inches or 30 to 40 centimeters is for the most part sufficient, potatoes are fine as you hill as they develop.

Raised Garden Bed Sizes

You just need your nursery bed to be raised to around 12 to 15 inches. The length can be whatever length suits and the width should be an agreeable reach for you to the inside from the two sides without venturing into the bed.

The stature of the bed ought to be whatever tallness suits you. And when you would prefer not to twist around while tending your nursery, at that point assemble your raised bed to an agreeable tallness that will permit you to tend the vegetables without the need to twist your back.

Raised nursery beds are perfect for those with handicaps or the old who think that its hard to bow down and all the more critically get up in the wake of bowing down.

And when you wish to manufacture your own raised beds, at that point your choices are many. You can utilize timber, solid squares, retainer divider paver squares, stone. In the case of utilizing timber, just use non-treated timber like a cedar as the treated timbers normally contain poisonous substances that can siphon out into the dirt and you will risk your vegetables taking up the poisons.

There are likewise units and instant raised bed vegetable gardens that you can buy and spare the time in building them yourself. Look at your neighborhood nursery providers or have a shop around on the web.

It is likewise conceivable to have this sort of nursery without strong sides. Start with a decent layer of rock for seepage and afterward hill up the dirt you wish to utilize, ensure you relax the ground underneath before putting down the dirt.

As an encompass for the bed you could utilize a thicker fringe of mulch as an edging. I would possibly do this if the pathways between the beds were not grass yet a mulch or rock with the goal that weeds or grasses couldn't discover their way into the developing territory.

The pathways can be an alluring and low support alternative as well, particularly in the event that you utilize a wood chip or bark mulch or something like deteriorated stone.

Some points

Raised bed vegetable nurseries are intended to be low upkeep. That implies by utilizing this framework, that is, adding your own dirt blend to the beds, the weeds, nuisances and ailments are everything except dispensed with.

Better seepage is another bit of leeway as having the bed raised permits the water to deplete away and not leave the plants water-logged.

Harvest turn is significant when developing vegetables. Basically, crop revolution implies not developing a similar vegetable two years straight in a similar spot.

With raised bed vegetable nurseries, you can have the beds whatever size you need. This size ought to be dictated by the size of your family or your vegetable needs.

So in the event that you are an individual living all alone or have a group of ten, your raised vegetable nursery can cook for your requirements.

You needn't bother with a major region to have a vegetable nursery utilizing the raised framework. And when you have a little yard or even a gallery, at that point you can utilize similar standards to develop your own one of a kind vegetables.

The best preferred position for you the plant specialist is, by utilizing this arrangement of raised bed vegetable cultivating it has been appeared, contrasted with the customary vegetable nurseries, to create almost twice as much in a littler region.

For whatever length of time that you follow the standards of raised bed planting then you can be developing and eating your own vegetables in the blink of an eye. That is the excellence of vegetable cultivating, your hold up is just merely weeks much of the time.

A few planters do it at little to no cost and use roughage bunches to encase their nursery. You can do that however your nursery bed will presumably just most recent a year. Wooden edges last more, and most digital books or nursery locales will discuss building a bed from cedar or pine. (Stone will obviously be all the more dependable, yet wood will do.)

Or on the other hand you can arrange from the site that sells the simple to-amass units for this reason. The primary method of building raised beds includes some elbow grease,but with it comes fulfillment; you would need to secure the secret sauce to assemble your raised bed:wood, blocks, concrete, stones.

The subsequent choice is to utilize the casing everything units which come in complete packs and you simply need to screw them together and introduce them in your porch region or the nursery. These units are made of composite wood that doesn't spoil effectively and they are light and smaller enough for little or large gardens.

There are various advantages to having a raised bed vegetable nursery. It will add structure and excellence to your nursery and make it a mess simpler to water your plants. Likewise the raised bed garden depletes impeccably, but since of the idea of the nursery bed you should utilize trickle water system or a sprinkler.

Another strong advantage is that you can pick which vegetables to plant, you see them growing up before your eyes and you can cull them whenever they are ready. You spare a considerable amount on vegetables that you would typically purchase from your nearby store. Having a raised bed vegetable nursery is likewise a decent reason for the family to work at something together and have a fabulous time!

Collect the produce after around two months,when the tomatoes and beans have expand pleasantly and rest languidly in their vines or cases holding back to be culled. After seven days you can plant again and begin growing an entirely different bunch of vegetables for your necessities.

The raised bed herb cultivating process is extraordinary compared to other planting methods that can be utilized and is picking up prominence consistently as it is a simpler method of cultivating yet different advantages additionally make it well known.

The raised bed cultivating method that is utilized can be used for developing different plants too. This is strategy which is very helpful for plant specialists in colder atmospheres. Fundamentally, the planter raises beds on a daintily raised stage than the real ground and the profundity of the nursery can be as much as required by the plant specialist. This additionally makes the nursery incredibly sorted out.

Raised nursery beds or nursery grower are perfect for little vegetable gardens or bloom gardens. Issues with weeds and soil compaction are kept under control with this sort of method. In addition, there is acceptable soil waste and the bugs like slugs and snails are kept from getting into your nursery. You can purchase instant grower or make them yourself without any problem.

As a plant specialist, and when your advantage is to set up a raised bed vegetable nursery, at that point you are positively on the correct page. You will discover all the data about the advantages and set up of a raised bed garden directly here.

Raised bed vegetable nurseries appreciate the accompanying advantages and it doesn't make a difference if your nursery bed is raised only a couple of inches or two or three feet.

Access to your nursery turns into a mess simpler when you utilize the raised bed method. Cultivating requires extended periods of time of difficult work on twisted knees and one approach to evade the strain is to utilize raised beds. Senior individuals can truly make the most of their cultivating exercises and the advantage of not twisting for a very long time to do their planting.

You can pick the best nature of soil accessible for your nursery and blend in the perfect measure of manures to furnish your plants with sound supplement rich soil. You can include the fertilizer and other natural issue to improve it before filling the grower. Further, there is no dirt compaction which implies a fluffier, non compacted, sound soil for your plants. Soil seepage is additionally generally excellent with raised beds.

Raised bed gardens make for better perceivability - you will think that its much simpler to detect that bug! With upgraded perceivability, taking great consideration of your nursery turns into much simpler.

Raised beds are a decent method to keep weeds from assaulting as there is constrained space for them to spread out. Weed control is a breeze when you utilize raised nursery beds.

The arranging of a raised bed vegetable nursery is surely not altogether different from arranging a customary vegetable nursery that you would have planted legitimately into the dirt in your nursery. First distinguish the area of your nursery, plants will require at any rate 5 hours of direct daylight and ensure there is acceptable soil seepage in the area you pick.

Attempt to keep your nursery quite far from the trees since roots can harm your nursery and furthermore conceal your plants, keeping them from getting immediate daylight. Raised nursery beds are typically about a foot higher than the encompassing soil level or you can utilize grower that will accept them as high off the ground as you need them. Grower stands are accessible in the nursery stores. What you have to guarantee when utilizing grower is that the dirt is in any event 2 feet deep for your nursery to flourish appropriately.

Imprint out the nursery limit utilizing shower paint or rope. At that point measure the space to comprehend what size grower to purchase. Purchase your manure, soil, compost and seeds in a single parcel for your nursery - will spare you going to and fro. Figure the measure of soil per sack to the area of your nursery. Nursery store partners are very much happy to assist you with your buys.

And when you assemble one it is a lot simpler to arrive at the plants or vegetables that you are developing. You can plan the bed to be as high or low as you wish. That, yet you can construct the holder in a spot that is anything but difficult to get to. This is the reason raised bed vegetable cultivating is extremely mainstream among senior residents and individuals in wheelchairs.

Another extraordinary thing about raised bed vegetable planting is expanded perceivability. You will have the option to see your create and guarantee that it is developing appropriately. It will likewise permit you to see things, for example, weeds and irritations a lot simpler. At the point when the nursery is raised, it will make it simpler for you to take phenomenal consideration of your nursery to guarantee sound and nutritious vegetables.

Being able to make your own dirt is maybe the greatest bit of leeway to raised bed vegetable cultivating. At the point when you manufacture a holder you will import your own dirt to make the bed. This permits you to pick top notch soil and blend it in with the right manures and fertilizer. You can invest energy inquiring about the best blend of manures and fertilizer to add to the dirt. The advantages will be a lot more advantageous vegetables or plants.

When you construct the compartment the exact opposite thing to choose is which vegetables you need to develop. Raised bed vegetable cultivating is a venture of time and cash, however it will likewise take care of you with better plants, more space and simpler access. That, yet raised bed gardens require considerably less support. The issue with weeds and keeping the zone developed is chopped down. You will be required to water the plants all the more regularly, however attaching a dribble water system framework is sufficiently simple. Simply make certain to assess the upsides and downsides of raised bed vegetable cultivating and settle on a choice that best suits you.

It is frequently a very disappointing time coming up for any cultivator whose plans incorporate plants that require great water waste, yet whose nursery is continually water logged. While there are numerous plants that do fine and dandy even in conditions with overabundance water, the opposite is likewise obvious. A similar water that makes a few assortments of blossoms sprout wonderfully rapidly slaughters off other bloom assortments. It is in this manner significant that any planter explore the water necessities of any plants, and match them with the nursery, before purchasing and planting, to guarantee a less distressing cultivating experience.

There is a simple method to test exactly how well the seepage in your nursery is. Burrow a little opening, around 30 cm profound, in the nursery. Fill that with water, and afterward leave it for a day or something like that. At the point when all the water has gone from the opening, fill it with water once more. In the event that this second filling of water has not vanished inside 12 hours or something like that, at that point the nursery has high water maintenance, or moderately poor waste. And when you are lamentable enough to have such a nursery, you should invest in more energy to guarantee great plant endurance and development for most plants.

One of the most famous methods of managing poor seepage in a nursery is using raised beds. The essential formula includes the making of a fringe for a bed, and afterward including manure and soil in enough amounts to raise it around 5 crawls over the remainder of the nursery. Indeed, even an alteration this little will add considerably to the waste for that particular fix.

There are contrasts in making a raised bed, contingent upon whether you are making it on a green territory, or over soil. A raised bed over a non-verdant territory is a generally basic undertaking. An outskirt or gatekeeper to hold the fertilizer and soil you use to make the bed is all you need. Numerous plant specialists prevail with regards to doing this with only two or three two by fours nailed together. When the outskirt is set up, simply include the correct mix of soil and fertilizer or compost. Recall that you may need to include more if any decay happens once you water your new raised bed.

Things are more muddled when you are building a brought bed up in a territory that as of now has grass. The most ideal path is to stamp out the border for your proposed raised bed, and cut out the turf around this edge. The grass then should be flipped over. While this seems like a basic strategy, care should be taken, to guarantee that the instrument you use is sufficiently sharp to cut the turf, so it tends to be flipped around. Moreover, it is educated to include a layer concerning straw, to keep the grass from becoming back up.

When this is done, soil and manure would then be able to be added to make the raised bed.

When you are content with your raised fix you can plant in it in the typical design. The one safety measure is that the underlying foundations of your new plants don't expand excessively far into the first soil level. The very quintessence of making a raised bed, is to diminish the measure of waterlogged soil that your plants' underlying foundations are in, so the shallower the better.

Numerous nursery workers report seeing quick upgrades in the wellbeing, and development of plants in raised beds, contrasted and those in ordinary water logged soil. While water is useful for plants, the more controlled measures in raised beds are better, and result in better plant prosperity. The possibility of making raised beds appears from the outset overwhelming for most plant specialists, yet the outcomes surely make the assignment an advantageous one. In the event that you don't know whether making a raised bed can improve your nursery, you can explore different avenues regarding a little fix of your nursery, and in the event that you see enhancements, increment the size of the raised patches.

Most nursery workers duplicate the business rancher and mastermind their vegetable nursery plants in long, level columns. This is the best technique when you're utilizing ranch apparatus, yet not in any way important for a little nursery. Rather than diving plants into long straight columns, a progressively profitable technique is to utilized raised beds.

Raised bed vegetable planting is a proven technique created more than a great many years. It is the primary way that families in China develop their own food. Maybe we can gain from their aggregate planting experience.

Lasting developing beds are raised somewhat over the ground. The raised beds are four feet across at the base and around 6 inches tall. This makes for a three foot wide developing surface at the highest point of the raised bed. Making the beds 25 feet in length will deliver a 100 square foot developing zone. This makes it simple to apply limestone or different supplements at a careful rate.

In the middle of the raised columns are ways where individuals can walk or sit to tend the plants. Ways are one foot wide and on either side of every way is an a couple of inch trough that gathers spillover. Gathering spillover in the troughs shields the ways from getting too sloppy on the grounds that the water remains in the planting beds. Better waste is one favorable position of the raised bed arrangement of developing food.

Raised beds likewise expand the developing season by permitting the dirt to heat up prior in spring and to remain hotter into late pre-winter. Somewhat because of the great waste gave by the nearness of the troughs, the raised beds can evaporate out and warm quicker than wet ground.

Strolling close to plants in an ordinary nursery hinders their development. In the raised bed strategy you just stroll on the ways where no plants are developing. This diminishes compaction in the developing region to nil taking into consideration better root development and better plant development. The ways are lasting ways and following a couple of years the dirt turns out to be compacted to such an extent that not weeds will develop there.

Since compaction in the developing beds isn't a difficult it requires less exertion to turn over the dirt every prior year planting. All you'll require is a scoop; no hardware is required. Contrasted with an ordinary nursery, utilizing raised beds will chop down the measure of time and exertion expected to till the nursery, prepare and water the plants, and evacuate weeds just because of less squandered space. You can rely on about a half decrease in the time required for these undertakings since you'll be just working with plants in the raised developing beds and not the pathways.

Raised bed planting guarantees more nourishment for less work and less contributions of water and compost. Those are sufficient motivations to check out them one year from now, however understand that raised beds additionally look very overall quite efficient. The developing territory can be sprinkled with blossoming plants to make the entire nursery a loosening up place rather than a spot to proceed to work.

Natural Gardening With Raised Beds

There are numerous best approaches natural in your nursery, however one way that permits you to do it with somewhat less upkeep, and somewhat more control is utilizing a raised bed garden. A raised bed garden is worked above or on the ground. It tends to be any shape or size that you can consider, however for the most part they are square or square shape fit as a fiddle and are between 6 to 12 crawls in tallness. And when you are building a vegetable nursery, I prescribe going 10 to 12 inches deep to give sufficient space for your vegetable roots. Basically every one of the a raised bed is, is a huge holder for your plants. The beds that I have in my nursery are 4 feet by 8 feet and 10 inches down.

I have discovered that there are three region's to focus your endeavors on when natural planting, soil the executives, weed the executives and nuisance control. As you may have speculated natural planting with raised beds falls into the "Dirt Management" zone. The greatest advantage of cultivating in these beds, is they let you control the specific soil you are utilizing. In the event that you are sadly enough to have poor soil on your property, planting with raised beds is the best decision for you. At the point when you assemble your raised bed ensure you put excellent soil from different sources, so you realize your plants have all the supplements they need.

And when you live in a chilly atmosphere, planting with raised beds permit you to begin prior on the grounds that since they are raised over the ground, they heat up snappier then customary nurseries. This gives you somewhat of a head start on your cultivating season. Another reward with them being raised, is you don't need to twist down as far to work in them.

Natural Gardening with raised beds additionally falls into the weed control zone of natural cultivating in light of the fact that since they are raised off the ground, it is more enthusiastically for weed seeds to discover their way into your nursery. Likewise, in the event that you have added a base to your crate, you have closed off any weed sprinters that would have made it into your nursery from underneath, which makes the nursery simpler to keep up after the underlying structure process. A base to your raised bed likewise assists with bug control, as it makes an obstruction that rodents and different nuisances can't get past.

At the point when you assemble your case, make a point to fabricate it so you can arrive at all pieces of the nursery all things considered. An individual can by and large arrive at 2 feet without requiring support, in the event that you are of a littler edge you should go a foot and a half. This implies you need to keep your beds from 3 to 4 feet in width. By remembering this you will never need to step on our dirt, this shields it from compacting which permits simpler plant developed and upkeep.

Useful points of raised bed cultivating

There are a few important points for the planter that utilizes the raised bed herb cultivating technique. The dirt contained in the raised nurseries will likewise be defrosted and warm a lot sooner than the dirt at the genuine ground level when the spring comes. This is on the grounds that the ice is at the ground level, while the beds are raised over the ground.

Moreover these brought beds permit planting up in territories which have poor soil quality. The beds are additionally more available than the real ground level. This likewise helps in improving the produce from the brought gardens up in contrast with the genuine ground itself. Those that develop the herb plants additionally utilize the mix of the raised nursery technique and on ground strategy. This aides in dragging out the developing season successfully.

Developing raised nurseries

For building the raised bed herb planting, there are not many materials that are required alongside some muscle power. And when you have, the labor, at that point it's a significant basic assignment to make the raised bed herb planting. To make the nursery, outlines should be built. The casings can be built from non-treated woods, blocks made of concrete and shakes. Utilizing railroad tracks or other treated woods for the herb nursery can present issues for the herbs.

The right elements of the casings should be taken a shot at, contingent upon the space accessible with the plant specialist. After the casings have been raised, it should be loaded up with topsoil, and other natural issue. Building a raised nursery is more costly than planting the herb garden in soil. Nonetheless, there won't be individuals stomping on over the nursery and it tends to be effectively kept up for quite a long time to come.

And when you are not a jack of all trades or lady, at that

point you can purchase corrogated type gardens and these are awesome and effectively transportable if needs • be.

Issues with the raised nurseries

The raised bed herb cultivating are perfect for restricted spaces. Nonetheless, the additional costs of building the edges and filling it with as much topsoil and other natural issue, for example, possible be a considerable amount toward the beginning of the nursery. The extents should be set out ahead of time; else it very well may be tedious when the edges should be modified.

What's the raised garden bed?

A raised garden bed (or simply "raised bed") is a large planting tub that sits above the ground and is filled with soil and plants. It is a box with no bottom or top—a container, really—that is put in a sunny spot and filled with good soil—to become a source of pride and enjoyment and a centrepiece of the garden.

Why should i build a raised garden bed?

The elevated beds have many advantages. Here are some of the reasons why you should consider using one: • garden tasks are made more accessible and more enjoyable thanks to less bending and kneeling. Save your knees and back from the pain and pressure of tending the garden!

• plant productivity is increased due to better drainage and deeper rooting.

• the raised beds are suitable for small areas where the traditional row garden can be too wild and unwieldy. Raised beds help keep things orderly and in order.

• planting in a raised bed gives you complete control of soil quality and material, which is especially important in areas where the current soil is rocky, nutrient-poor or weed-ridden.

• the raised beds allow for a longer growing season, as you can work the soil more quickly in the spring in frost-hardened areas, or turn the bed into a cold layer in the fall.

• fewer weeds are seen in raised beds as the bed is elevated away from nearby plants and is lined with disease-free and weed-free soil.

• the raised beds for more natural square-foot gardening and companion planting.

Choosing the right wood for raised beds

Many people are worried about the health of their wooden frames. First, be sure that cca-treated wood is prevented, as it was known, from leaching arsenic. There are several ways to ensure that the wood lasts: • standard pressure-treated timber sold today has a combination of chemicals used to prevent wet soil from rotting and weather from rotting. While pressurized is certified as safe for organic cultivation, some people have concerns about using it, and there is a range of environmentally friendly alternatives.

• more costly woods, such as cedar, contain natural oils that resist rotting and make them much more durable. They're more expensive to buy, but they're going to last a lot of years.

• choosing thicker boards can make the wood last longer. For example, 2-inch-thick locally grown larch will last for ten years, even without treatment.

• avoid the use of rail links, because they can be handled with créosote, which is poisonous.

Alternatives to wood include blocks of concrete or bricks. Bear in mind. However, that concrete will raise the ph of the soil over time, and you will need to change the earth accordingly to create your best garden.

How big will your raised bed be?

• first, you need a place with a low ground level and the right amount of sunlight (6 to 8 hours a day). This is expected to narrow down the choices a bit.

• as far as the size of the bed is concerned, 4 feet is a growing width. Lumber is always cut in 4-foot intervals, so you do want to be able to reach the garden without reaching the house. Making the bed too big would make it difficult to reach the centre, making weeding and harvesting a pain.

• it's not as critical as time. Typical plots are typically 4 feet wide by 8 feet long or 4 feet wide by 12 feet long. Make your bed as long as you want it or create several raised beds for different crops.

• the depth of the bed can vary, but 6 inches of soil should be the minimum. Most garden plants need at least 6 to 12 inches for roots, so 12 inches is ideal.

Preparing the site for raised bed

• before you lay down a bed, break up and loosen the soil underneath the garden fork so that it is not compacted. Go 6 to 8 inches down. For better rooting, some gardeners prefer to remove the top layer (about the depth of a spade), dig another layer, and then return the top layer and mix the soil layers.

• if you are planning to position your raised bed in an area currently occupied by a lawn, put down a cardboard sheet, a tarp, or a piece of landscaping cloth to destroy the grass first. After around six weeks (or less depending on the weather), the grass will be dead and much more natural to cut.

Building a raised garden bed

 • place wooden stakes at every corner (and every few feet for longer beds) to support wooden beds. Place the inside of the bed so that the stakes are less visible.

• lower the stakes about 60 per cent (2 feet) to the ground and leave the remainder of the stakes exposed above ground.

• check that the stakes are high enough to be on the ground at the same height, otherwise that you have uneven beds.

• set the lowest boards a few inches below ground level.

Check that it's perfect.

• using galvanized nails (or screws) to secure the boards on the stakes.

• install some additional rows of boards, securing them to the stakes,

Soil for raised garden beds

The soil blend that you put in your raised bed is the most crucial ingredient. More gardens fail or collapse due to bad soil than almost anything else.

• fill the beds with a mixture of topsoil, compost and other organic material, such as manure, to give your plants a nutrient-rich atmosphere (see recipes below). Learn more about soil alteration and soil preparation for planting.

• note that the soil in the raised bed would dry up more quickly. During the spring and fall, this is perfect, but in the summer, apply grass, mulch, or hay to the top of the soil to help it hold moisture.

• regular watering with raised beds will be necessary, particularly in the early stages of plant development. Otherwise, elevated beds would require minimal maintenance.

• 4 bags (2 cubic feet each) of topsoil (note: avoid using topsoil from your yard as it can contain weeds and pests) • 2 pails (3 cubic feet each) of coconut coir (to increase drainage) • 2 bags (2–3 cubic feet each) of composted or composted cow manure • 2-inch layer of shredded leaves or grass clippings (grass clippings should be herbicide-free f) within a matter of minutes, you can build a garden plan right on your screen.

The garden planner has a 'made garden bed' option. It also has a unique square foot gardening (sfg) function, which involves dividing the bed into squares to make the organizing of your garden much more straightforward (see photo above).

Whichever garden you pick, the garden planner will show you the number of crops that fit into each area so that you don't waste seed or overcrowd. There's even a companion planting device that lets you plant vegetables that grow together and avoid plants that hinder each other.

Check our garden planner with a free 7-day trial — a ton of time to plan your first garden! If you like the garden planner, we hope you can sign up. Otherwise, it's enough time to play around and give it a go

Plot out your garden

Good soil, good sunlight, and proper drainage are essential criteria for a productive vegetable garden, but preparing your garden should not be a last-minute thought. Each garden —

and every gardener — is unique, so make a garden personalized to your space and needs.

For example, a 100-square-foot garden (10x10 feet) will quickly grow a large variety of vegetables. Bisecting it with two narrow paths shapes four beds that are easy to access and enter. (one column, one square foot.)

Chapter Four

Planning Your Gardening

30 Raised Garden Beds Plans & Ideas You Can Build In A Day

30 raised garden beds plans & ideas you could create a day planting on raised garden beds offers many advantages compared to planting on the grass. But the most important thing is that you can grow a garden, even in the soil field.

When you have issues with your back, the garden beds may be the ideal remedy. Also, check out our post about diy garden beds made of scrap wood.

But there's one drawback: you have to create a bed before you can start a garden. Although garden beds are simple construction, there's still extra work to be done.

So, to make your work easier, we've gathered 76 raised garden bed plans that you can create easily. If you need any ideas or directions, this list is certainly going to be helpful.

How to build your free raised garden beds (right way) while garden beds are not a permanent construction, you certainly don't want to move or remove them when you put them on the field especially after you've added soil and plants to it.

That's why there are four things to remember before you start building:

1. Plan where you're going to put your beds. Usually, you'd like the sunniest place if you are going to grow plants that require shade.

2. Plan how many beds you need. A big bed is more cost-effective than a few smaller beds. Yet depending on what you're going to grow, lower beds might be a safer option. It's better to bring identical plants and 'real friends' together in one room.

3. Consider the size of your bed, please. Don't build a mattress that is more than three feet wide; it's easier to handle. But it may be as long as you want it to be. If you plant smaller plants like herbs, you can not need large beds.

4. Prepare the content that you need. Most people use wood; it's cheaper, durable, and light. You can use recycled pallet wood for even less expensive products. Yet if you need a more permanent solution, you can make use of concrete.

Now, let's continue with the free raised garden bed plans.

30 free diy raised garden bed plans

1. Two tier garden bed this elevated garden bed has an exceptional design. In reality, it's two-tier. It's supposed to have a step-step appearance.

The very cool thing about this concept is that you can plant it on both levels. So, if you've got anything you'd like to plant that could be higher, then plant it on the bottom floor.

So you can plant smaller plants or flowers on the second floor, and they'll still be visible and get plenty of sunlight.

2. The no-frills garden bed so maybe you're not looking for a specific design. Perhaps you just want something that keeps your plants coordinated and clean, but it's also going to be easy to create.

Okay, go no further than that. This garden bed is a simple square with simple design instructions. It's not getting any easier than that.

So, if you're new to carpentry, this could be a decent entry-level raised garden bed project for you. And it's going to add a beautiful look to your yard, too.

3. Easy cedar garden boxes

When you have a fenced yard, these boxes are going to look amazing. In reality, this is one of my favourite traditional garden beds. The explanation is that there are two boards high, which means that gardening in them is much easier on your back.

Yet i love the clean feel of it all, too. And the wood of cedar is not too bad either. So, if you're looking for an organized way to plant your flowers or vegetables, add those beauties to your backyard. They're sure to make your yard pop.

4. Landscaping timbers garden beds

So have i ever mentioned that i have a 'thing' to do with landscaping? Ok, i do that. They are typically inexpensive and have a way to add order and simple elegance to an environment that was once messy and unattractive.

How will the results for your garden beds be different? You stack these beauties together and, once again, you have an organized room for whatever vegetable or flower you want to grow in that field.

5.growing bed with benches

These are perfect looking garden beds. Beyond the beauty that wood brings to the picture, let's talk about the functionality of these raised beds.

First of all, they're pretty tall. It is similar to a less bending and a happier, less tired back. But instead, they do have tables, which means you've got places to keep your tools or even a spot to relax while you're working in your flowers.

5. Fenced garden bed

Do you have grizzly vegetable predators around your house? Yeah, me too, man! We've got rabbits and squirrels everywhere. They're all going with the territory when you live in the middle of the woods, right?

Well, if you've got that question, then maybe this garden bed is just for you. It's three boards high, and it's perfect for the ease of working in your backyard. But it also has a fence around your garden area. It could help keep your unwanted guests out of what you planted.

7.diy garden enclosure

Okay, don't let the photo get you confused. What you've got here are three raised beds and a standing area. They're all enclosed by a net and a fence.

It is excellent news for your flowers and plants, as the enclosure ensures that they are less likely to be disturbed by any unwelcome visitors. So again, if you have a pest problem, you may want to consider giving this enclosure ago.

8,garden enclosure

Here's another garden enclosure. Isn't that wonderful? It offers your plants and flowers an excellent place to grow and adds a little rustic charm to the beautiful forest.

I also love how good it looks to grow a small variety of what you might like in your backyard. So, if you've got any plants that pests are going out of their way to go after this might be a safe place to grow them successfully.

9. Raised bed planter stand

This is a creative idea if you want to grow something new or pretty and place it in a smaller area. I could see that working well on my front porch. What a beautiful way to show off your flowers without getting them to fall to the ground.

The smart idea is if you're a homesteader in the building. It would be a perfect addition that could easily fit on the balcony and grow a lot of fresh herbs and vegetables.

10. Elevated bed

With legs, i like this idea of a high garden bed. Again, let's assume that you live in an apartment or that you want to develop something in a smaller space. This high garden bed helps you to do that.

Perhaps more so, it's waterproof, too. And if you don't like the idea of anything permanent, then in this situation, you don't have to think about it. When you decide you like it somewhere else, you just have to switch it from year to year.

11. I like these raised beds, diy raised garden beds.

They're great. What i love even more is that they seem to be very easy to build. I claim this because the lady who wrote this post had never designed garden beds before, and she made those beds look gorgeous.

So, if you're new to building garden beds, this might be a good tutorial for you. Her list of directions is elementary to read, and so is her list of materials. You may find yourself having these beds built in no time at all.

12. Puppy evidence garden beds

Do you have a dog that likes to dig? Especially in your beds in the garden? Sure, i, too. I can sense the pain. My dog seems to think that if it's planted in one of the gardens, it's her job to dig it all up. I mean, how else would she get to sunbathe and roll in the dirt if the nasty plants remain in her way?

So, if you find yourself in this boat, maybe these garden beds will help you out. They're more prominent, and it's hard for most dogs to dig through them. I'd presume you'd be pretty safe unless you're like me and you have athletic dogs who will enjoy their regular entertainment jumping on top of these things.

13. Elevated garden bed

This is a bigger version of our leg garden bed. It's mostly a large box with the legs under it. This is a perfect concept as it makes it impossible for pests to find their way into your plants this way.

It's also a smart concept, because think about how much

simpler it is to grow, weed, and harvest when you don't have to bend over. Considering that my days during the summer are packed with a lot of pots and ends with aching back, this makes this raised garden bed look all the better for me.

14. The cheap raised garden bed

I like this garden bed and tutorial. Why? Why? And not only is it stunning, but it also provides advice about how to make it more budget-friendly.

So, if you're looking for a way to add subtle beauty to your backyard while growing tons of plants, then this is a perfect project to take on.

15. Striped garden bed

Such a simple addition to the traditional raised garden bed that gives an esthetic look! A brilliant way to add a little elegance to your garden!

It is an easy project to execute, and it will look fantastic in your front yard!

16. The square foot garden bed

This garden bed is exclusive. Consider for a moment that you don't want an exceedingly large garden. You just need a small room to cultivate a few vegetables that you've enjoyed in the warmer months.

Ok, if that's you, this garden bed is right up your alley. It is a raised bed with a frame laid over it, which delegates certain positions for specific vegetables. It's a perfect way to plan a small garden.

17. Diy tiered herb gardens

This herb garden is beautiful. Again, it's a lovely way to grow herbs that you'll use without raising an eyebrow or taking up a lot of space.

The herb garden will be a perfect addition to the front porch or the back patio. This would offer a fresh look to every sitting area, and this would also be a comfortable location that would make it easier to take care of them.

18. Hoop garden bed

This raised garden bed has an added feature which makes it incredibly cold. So you plant your seeds or plants, but then you encounter the freeze. How are you doing later?

Ok, if you've got this excellent garden bed, the solution is just to lower the cover. This lid will shield your plants from frost, while also giving you the chance to plant a little earlier or grow a little later in the season.

19. Tyre garden beds

If you're on a budget or just like a look of unique stuff, this garden bed may be for you. It's always easy to find old tractor tires for little to no cost.

Okay, what you've got to do is spread the tires out and fill them with dirt. Then plant your seedlings or seeds, and you've got your own garden space.

20. Curved raised beds

If you're someone who likes to add a little flair to your design, you might like this raised garden bed option.

They're bringing several beds together to create a 'u' shape. This provides a very cool design while carrying a lot of your plants closer together, making it a little easier to take care of them.

21. The ultimate garden bed

This garden bed tutorial has been built to cover you. Whether you're new to building garden beds or growing plants, they're going through every step you need.

The design of this garden bed is simple, but it also shows you how to attach a protective cover for frost or birds that is always handy to help give your crop a chance to fight.

22. Planter box

This is a simple but beautiful template for a planter box.

They put their table in front of their fence. It's an excellent height that makes it a little easier for you to take care of your plants.

After building a simple foundation, it just has to be filled with soil and plant the plants you like. It's a beautiful and straightforward way to add a bit of colour and life to your backyard.

23. Pallet planter

Because you do know if there's anything that can be made,

there's possibly a way to build it out of a pallet. I'm a fan of items made out of pallets, of course, because it's a durable, cheap material that's pretty easy to reach.

This planter is higher off the ground, making it easier to use. Yet it also has a fantastic rustic feel that brings a little extra appeal to the yard it's in.

24. Herb planter

I love the planters of herbs. They look great, and they will brighten up any place they're in. In particular, i love this one with the first table legs that accompany the raised bed.

The elevation is another advantage of growing herbs in an elevated position. It makes working on your herbs enjoyable, and it's no longer a backbreaking task.

It's 25. Raised garden bed benches

Would you like to add these garden beds to your yard while providing some extra seating space? If this is the case, this style is for you. Imagine sitting in your yard, surrounded by beautiful flowers and plants.

Not to mention when it came time to weed or harvest, you might sit down when you're working, which makes for a more comfortable and enjoyable experience.

26. Sleeper garden bed

This is an innovative diy project that uses recycled rail ties or sleepers as a frame for your new garden bed.

A clean, durable and practical look. However, the diy project can't get any simpler than this!

27. Cement block raised garden beds

They had to be listed. I love these garden beds because they're what fills my backyard fence.

We've decided to go with these garden beds because they're cheap and easy to put together. Mostly, you're going to lay them down where you like them and fill them up. And i do love the feel of them.

28. Natural wood garden bed

Have you recently completed a project that involved clearing some of the lands? So now you've got a lot of spare twigs, so limbs left over? Okay, don't burn it or throw it away.

Why? Why? Because with a little framing, you can use the limbs to create a natural planting frame. It's exceptional and practically doesn't cost anything to produce. It is a bonus for this project.

29. I love upcycling, dresser herb garden.

It is so fascinating to see all the various ways in which you can reuse an object that is no longer being used for its original purpose.

Okay, there's no difference in this herb garden. We just took out the drawers of the dresser and removed the ashes. Then the herbs were rooted in them. It gives an exceptional look, but it's also very sleek.

30. Raised garden beds for vegetables

This tutorial is about making cheap raised beds help your family grow more of their food. Building your diet is a significant part of living a more self-sustaining lifestyle and saving money.

So, making your garden beds that add a beautiful touch is just an investment that will hopefully save you a few bucks down the road.

Chapter Five

What To Grow And What Not To Grow In Your Raised Beds

There's nothing more satisfying in life than the crunch of fresh vegetables grown right outside your house. If you're a gardening newbie or a seasoned green thumb, raised beds are a perfect way to make that happen.

Such simple structures offer some significant advantages: in the first place, the soil can be tailored to your needs, because you will be filling your beds rather than using what is already usable. This dirt is often covered by walls, which ensures that it is never stepped on and compacted and thus absorbs excess water quickly. Eventually, the soil in these beds warms up faster in the spring, giving you a longer growing season.

On a boat, huh? Now you just have to decide what to build—while the raised beds are perfect for almost anything to improve, these are the real stars that rise above the rest.

1.root vegetables

When you grow plants because of their roots, it is necessary to have complete control over the soil. Raised beds can be lined with the ideal ground, free from rocks, mud and debris, which may impede the growth of roots or cause misshapen veggies. Carrots, beets, radishes and parsnips grow in the loose, rock-free soil where they have space to spread.

2.leafy greens

Such as lettuce, spinach and kale work well in raised beds, and these cool-weather crops need to be planted as soon as you can get a trough into your soil. The fact that the land in the raised beds warms faster than the ground means that you can get going sooner and have a few sweet harvests before the summer hits. Leafy greens always hate soggy roots, so your bed's fast-draining soil ensures that your lovely lettuce will never have to stay in the water for too long.

3. Onions

There are three reasons why onions are the ideal vegetable to grow in raised beds: they love quick-draining soil, they need a lot of organic matter, and they need a long growing season. By default, the land in the raised beds can be tailored to your needs, so if you know you're going to plant onions in the garden, you can be sure to add a lot of compost.

Note: onions grown from seeds can take more than 100 days to reach maturity. And if you live anywhere with four seasons, you're going to want to give these babies the longest time you can handle in the garden. The colder soil in the raised bed gives a head start to your onions!

4. Tomatoes

Tomatoes are heavy feeders that need nutrient-dense soil to thrive. And, as with onions, you're going to want to tailor this soil to have extra compost. The only downside to growing tomatoes in raised beds is that it's difficult for cages and stakes to stand up in the loose soil.

5. Potatoes

Potatoes not only grow well in a raised bed, but they're also much more comfortable to harvest in this way. These plants benefit from the rocky soil around the shoots as they grow; you can easily hold your hills in the raised bed. You can even build a mattress that you can attach to as your plants grow.

Potatoes do need loose, loamy soil, which drains well. They grow best when they can spread quickly in the land, and this loose soil will prevent them from rotting. Potato crops grown in raised beds tend to have higher yields with larger tubers.

These are just some of the crops that are going to grow well in a raised bed. While these are the crops that grow most quickly, with careful planning, you can also have success growing vineyards vertically on the trellises. And now that you know what your raised bed can do, it's time to get out there and get your hands dirty!

Chapter Six

Basics: Gardening In Raised Beds Greenhouse.

Attractive cedar beds are an asset to your landscape. Build perimeter gardens, spice up your entry, grow food in your front yard, screen your eyes.

There's more food in less space. You can bring the plants closer together so that every square inch is productive. And small-scale gardening methods, such as succession planting and vertical supports, ensure that every square inch of space is used.

Plant sooner than that

. Excess water drains better, and the soil heats up faster in spring than in-ground beds. Specialized covers and garden fabric help you get started earlier.

Better land.

A productive vegetable garden is based on good soil. For a raised bed, you start fresh for the perfect mix of land—even if the area on your site is terrible.

More weeds.

Since the raised beds are densely planted, weeds have little space for growing. And when they find space, it's easy to pull them out of the loose, fertile soil.

Easier management of the disease

. It's easier to control insects and remove animal pests than long rows of gardens. Beds with row fabrics or unique covers can be conveniently covered.

Align the soil with the plants.

Fill the beds with soil that is suited to the plants. Do you want to grow blue hydrangeas, for example? Upon planting, mix the soil acidifier in the land.

Less stretching to stretch.

Deep root raised beds are 15" high, so you bend less while planting, caring for, and harvesting plants. Choosing raised bed gardener's supply provides a wide variety of raised beds, from aluminium corner kits for which you supply your timber, too full raised bed kits in cedar, composite wood, recycled plastic and galvanized steel. You can also find raised beds for non-bend gaga. In general, the more soil depth your plants have, the more freely their roots can grow. Additional soil often retains extra moisture, and deeper raised beds may need less frequent watering.

A raised bed may be constructed on bad or compacted soil, or even on concrete. If that's the condition you've got, buy the deepest bed you can afford. A depth of 10-12 "is optimal. Bear in mind that the deeper the bed, the more soil you'll need to fill. Use the soil calculator to decide how much soil you'll need. How many raised beds do you have? If your room or time is restricted, you may want to start with only one. If you're trying to grow a lot of your fresh vegetables, you'll probably need at least three or four. This should enhance the drainage and moisture conservation of the raised beds. It also ensures that even with a 5"-high raised bed, your plants may assume they're growing in a 12-18" deep bed—ample space for carrots, potatoes, full-size tomato plants, and most of the other vegetables you'd ever want to grow.

If you're going to fill more than one raised bed, you may want to buy your soil in bulk — a cubic foot or a cubic yard. Use the soil calculator to measure the total amount of dirt required for every bed.

• 60 per cent topsoil

• 30 per cent compost

• 10 per cent potting soil (a soilless mix containing peat moss, perlite or vermiculite) • bear in mind that the proportions are estimated as the soil content varies from source to source. For example, if the calculator specifies. Four hundred forty-four cubic yards of soil for your bed, go ahead and buy a half yard.

• if you do not have access to topsoil content, an appropriate alternative will be a 50-50 mix of soilless growing medium (often referred to as "potting soil") and compost. If you want to apply peat moss to the surface, it should not be more than 20% of the total mix. Peat moss is naturally acidic and not a suitable medium for growing vegetables.

• **what to grow**

• fill your garden with the kind of vegetables you want to eat. If you're heavy on salads, plant head lettuce, lettuce cutting combination, cherry tomatoes, cucumbers and carrots. If you enjoy cooking, plant onions, peppers, leeks, potatoes and herbs. Seek to include at least one new crop. Discovery is half a fun thing.

• planting in an elevated bed is all about optimizing productivity. The goal is to produce as much food as possible while avoiding the urge to pinch too many plants. Overcrowded plants never achieve their full potential because they are stressed by poor air circulation and competition for water, nutrients and root space.

• our kitchen garden planner offers planting instructions to help you arrange your plants properly. Optimum spacing can vary slightly depending on the different plant varieties as well as the growing conditions. A bush of watermelon, such as sugar baby, has 3 ft. To 4 ft. Of vines, while the vines of a full-size melon, such as ruby, can be 15 ft. Long. Similarly, in texas, tomato plants are often more than 7 feet tall, but in vermont, they typically peak at 4 feet. Through practice, you can slowly acquire a sense of how much space each form of plant requires

• it is also essential to consider how the growth habit of each plant (bushy, climbing, trailing) would affect its neighbours in the same room. Planting lettuce next to carrots is delicate; planting lettuce next to a spreading cucumber plant may be a concern. Stakes, ladders and cages can help prevent unruly plants from interfering with neighbours. We can also make the garden cleaner and more manageable.

• while most of the vegetables you want to grow may be started directly from seed in the greenhouse, in many cases it's safer to start with a plant. Beginning with a plant, the harvest time is typically shortened by a month or more. In cold regions where the growing season may be less than 100 days, a tomato or pepper plant that has started in the seed garden does not have time to mature until frost. If you put in only one or two plants of a specific type of vegetable (such as broccoli or tomatoes), often it makes more sense to buy a few plants than to invest in a whole packet of seeds.

• vegetables that can be planted directly from the seed garden include root crops such as carrots and beets, beans, peas, corn, cucumbers, squash and salad greens. In some instances, these crops are sown directly because they do not rotate well, so it is better to sow the seeds where they can grow. In the case of salad greens, which germinate well and multiply, it is more economical to purchase a packet of seeds than to buy several six-packs of lettuce seedlings.

• potatoes can be started from seed, but almost nobody does. It's much quicker and easier to grow a new potato plant from a tuber rather than a grain. Onions may be placed into the garden as seeds, but more often they go in as plants or as "packages" which are simply tiny mature onions from the previous growing season. For more detail on selecting seeds, seedlings or sets, see rising onions. Garlic and shallots are commonly planted in games as well. When young plants, leeks go into the garden. Some herbs should be planted, others (cilantro and dill) should be seeded where they are to be grown.

When to plant there are many things to consider when determining when to plant a garden. The first is the sort of plant that you're bringing in. Some plants, including lettuce and broccoli, can withstand cold weather. Others, such as basil and tomatoes, are likely to be harmed or destroyed by temperatures below 40 degrees. Please refer to our vegetable encyclopedia for the best time to plant every crop.

Many essential factors include frost dates and soil temperature. For planting zones 3 to 6, the primary growing season is between the first and last frost days. Cold-sensitive plants must not be permitted to enter the garden until the danger of frost has passed. This typically falls somewhere between march and may, depending on your through a location. If you don't know your rising district, check the map of the usda region.

If you garden in zones 8-10, heat—not frost—may decide your planting dates. Warm-climate gardeners often plant in the fall rather than in the spring to reduce midsummer sun. Others are set up for two planting cycles per year: early autumn and late winter

Soil temperature is also an essential aspect of planting time. Many plants grow at a moderate soil temperature of 60 to 70 degrees f. Others, such as peas and spinach, germinate well and grow just fine in the cold (45 degrees f.) Soil. Others, such as aubergines and melons, do not germinate or grow appropriately unless the land is above 60 degrees f. Planting the vegetable encyclopedia provides suggestions for each crop

Many crops, including tomatoes, peppers, squash and corn, are typically planted only once per growing season. Other vegetables, such as salad greens, root crops, peas and beans, can be planted and harvested early and then cultivated for a second harvest later in the season. The plant encyclopedia has crop-specific recommendations for planting (and replanting) to help you optimize yield.

Tending your garden intensively holds weeds to a minimum. You may need to weed a little every week in early spring, but your weeding chores should be done by midsummer. When weeds grow, you'll want to remove them quickly so that your vegetable plants don't fight for moisture, nutrients and root space.

The soil in the raised bed does not dry out as quickly as it does in a typical garden. The sides of the bed help to preserve moisture and the plants shade the soil to reduce evaporation. Once the plants are well developed, your watering tasks should be minimal except in hot weather and dry seasons. See the watering section below for more information.

Crops that grow for three or four months to mature typically benefit from a second, mid-season application of fertilizer. Almost all vegetables value a monthly dose of water-soluble fertilizer, particularly one that includes humic acid, seaweed and fish emulsion. Such water-soluble nutrients are quickly consumed by plants and help keep them alive during the watering season. In an ideal world, mother nature will provide an inch of rain every week to keep our vegetables and flowers perfectly content. Since that probably won't happen, it's up to us to make sure our plants get the water they need to live on.

A rain gauge will help you keep track of how much rain has fallen, but that's just part of the story. Various forms of soil have different water keeping capabilities. The clay-based ground holds onto the water since any small part of the clay has a lot of surface area for the water to collect. Sandy soil, with its more massive particles, helps water to flow through easily. Healthy loamy soil retains some moisture but is also well-drained

Adding compost to the soil increases its ability to supply the right amount of water to your plants. Think of sandy soil as a wire basket full of golf balls: turn the hose on and the water flows in. Using compost is like adding sponges — water is still flowing through, but some are contained in the sponges. Compost also helps to improve clay soils by aerating them and providing better drainage. Plants consume oxygen from their roots and will drown if the soil stays soggy for weeks at a time. Raised beds and compost will help to prevent this from occurring.

The easiest way to track soil moisture is by your hands. When you put a finger down into the dirt, it's supposed to feel mildly moist – like a sponge that has been wrung out. Don't just touch the surface; bring your fingertips down to the root zone (3 "deep or so deep) at least once a week.

Plants will wilt during the heat of the day in hot weather. It is not necessarily a sign that they are devoid of moisture. For certain instances, it is merely a way for the plant to reduce the loss of moisture through its leaves. Checking the soil is telling the real story.

Intensive planting in a raised bed garden minimizes the loss of moisture. Plants shade the soil surface and help shield each other from the wind. Mulching around plants with 2-3 "of shredded leaves or straw is another efficient way to preserve moisture and add organic matter to the soil. When you know that your garden needs water, there are a variety of choices. A watering wand can provide quite a bit of water quickly and bring it right where you want it. Too busy with water during the week? Going on holiday in august? Buy a watering device to get it right where you want it.

Chapter Seven

Planting And Maintaining Crops In Raised Bed Gardens

5 Tips For Improving Your Raised Bed Garden Soil

Wondering how often, or even better yet, do you improve the soil in raised beds? You are thoroughly persuaded of the advantages of raised garden beds, and you could have been planting in raised beds for years.

If you're new to raised bed gardening or you're an increased bed gardening pro, we've got some gardening tips below on built bed soil maintenance. In a way, raised beds are like large containers. When you deplete soil nutrients in one or more growing seasons, you need to restore them. Sure, organic fertilizers are a smart thing to add in the spring. Yet they're not the full solution to improving the consistency of your soil.

Through properly preserving the soil in the raised beds, you won't have to remove it every few years. Unless your plants develop a soil-borne disease, you don't need to change your raised bed soil at all — just keep it! And what are you doing to keep the soil safe in raised beds? Below are a few tips:

1. Add compost

Compost is just not ready for spring bed preparation! In the fall, add compost to your raised beds. Compost is a perfect way to finish the planting season in raised beds. Because this compost is going to stay on the couch all winter, it doesn't have to be broken down. The composting process can occur on the raised bed. Besides, it's a great way to clean up the yard from fall yard wastes. Spread a couple of inches of compost on the bed, and then cover with mulch. The mulch will protect the soil from harsh winter weather, keeping the nutrients in the raised bed.

2, use soil amendments

Soil amendments are mixed with soil to improve soil quality in raised beds. As to precisely what soil amendments do to the land will depend on what kind of soil amendment you are using. You might want to consider using soil amendments to increase the soil's nutrients or to change the soil's physical structure, often called tilth. Simply put, it's the texture of the land. Let's say, for example, your soil in your raised bed is drying out too fast. Or, maybe you didn't use the right soil mixture in the first place. Possibly your soil had too much sand in it, making water drain quickly through the land before the plants have a chance to absorb it.

You can correct the soil by adding a soil amendment, like compost, rich in organic matter. The organic matter will retain moisture in the ground. On the flip side, if the soil is keeping too much water, you can mix greensand with the earth, which helps water drain more efficiently.

Here's a list of organic soil amendments you might want to look into to improve your raised bed soil quality: vermiculite (worm castings), compost, coir, greensand, grass clippings, cornmeal, alfalfa meal, lava sand, straw and kelp meal.

3.plant a cover crop

When thinking about replenishing nutrients in raised beds, don't forget about cover crops. Cover crops aren't just for large scale farmers looking for weed suppression. They will benefit raised beds for the backyard gardener, too.

Cover crops aerate the soil, especially if you plant a cover crop with a deep root system like alfalfa. The root system will pull nutrients deep in the land to the surface, which will make nutrients readily available when it comes to planting time. A few weeks before planting time, till the cover crop into the soil. This increases organic matter, building healthier soil and boosting nutrients.

4. Try lasagna gardening

 Lasagna gardening, sometimes called no-till gardening or sheet composting, is another great tip for improving soil conditions, and it's also a fantastic way to create a raised bed. So, whether you're looking to start from scratch or work on an existing raised bed garden, you can improve your soil conditions from the get-go. As your soil is gets depleted in your raised bed over time, you keep adding layers as you would in a lasagna garden, by sheet composting and completely renovate your soil from the top down.

5. Prepare raised beds for the winter

 Don't forget the end of the garden season is an excellent time for just a few simple steps for soil maintenance. It's kind of like closing up shop for the winter. That is if you aren't in an area of the country where you can grow year-round.

Chapter Eight
Materials For Raised Garden Beds

1.wood

This is possibly the most common material for the construction of raised beds, and perhaps one of the least costly. Using naturally rot-resistant woods such as cedar or redwood, and avoid toxin-containing woods such as creosote-soaked rail links. Pressure-treated lumber is treated with quaternary alkaline copper, which the epa considers healthy for food crops. Still, you might also want to line your beds with weed barrier fabric to prevent the soil from coming into contact with the wood.

Pros: wood beds are comfortable to build, and the material is readily available in most areas. They work well for traditional and more modern gardens, depending on the nature and layout of the beds. Wooden raised beds are the ideal project for ardent diyers. Wood is also one of the most cost-effective ways to create raised beds.

Cons: wood doesn't last forever, so you'll need to fix it at some point. Nevertheless, untreated wood will continue for some years (up to 10) without any visible rot, and treated wood can last longer.

Price: depending on the size of your bed, cedar or redwood can price up to $150 per bed; the amount of compressed wood is $75 to $100.

Hire a local carpenter to build upholstered wood beds

1.concrete

 The use of urban landscape features such as concrete has increased in recent years. What used to seem ordinary and modest can now be fashionable and even trendy, making concrete a very versatile and attractive addition to most styles of gardens.

Pros: concrete walls can last forever when properly built. These can also fit well in traditional, contemporary or even global styles (think spanish courtyard or mexican concrete) and can be tinted to complement, match or contrast with home and other structures.

Cons: concrete can be costly, and, in most situations, it is not a diy job.

.cost: materials are relatively cheap, but labour is more expensive, so the total cost is not always at the low end of the choices. Expect to pay around $30 per square foot, but that cost could increase dramatically if you have issues, such as a sloping yard, that makes it more challenging to prepare for work.

Find a concrete specialist to pour out the raised beds

3.masonry

Masonry's raised beds are the garden world camels. They can comfortably fit into almost any kind of garden, depending on the type of rock you use. If you're a handy diyer, you may be able to complete a project like this on your own, but most homeowners would prefer to employ a masonry crew to build the beds properly.

Pros: masonry can be a permanent addition, and materials are available almost everywhere. The masonry raised beds arc lovely and can be designed to fit in with or even suit the exterior of your house.

Cons: the artefact can be very costly, depending on the type of rock.

Cost: most masons charge a linear or square foot; for raised beds, you plan to pay $5 to $10 per square foot or more if you select a higher-priced rock.

4.cinderblock

Raised beds made of cinderblock can be built in a variety of different ways. Cinderblocks can simply be stacked at the desired height of the bed, or they can be mortared in place and then provided a more stylish finish with surface treatment and capped tops, as seen here. The former is much more rustic and cheap, while the latter is more sophisticated and more valuable.

Pros: cinderblock is very cheap and readily available; you can purchase it from home improvement stores or construction supplies stores. Based on the design, it can suit a wide variety of styles, from rustic to industrial to elegant. It's pretty robust, too, so it's going to remain in place for several years.

Cons: the individual pieces are enormous, making it difficult to do this solo project.

Cost: there are a few different types of cinderblock; materials alone cost from $9 to $15 per square foot. When you employ a specialist and install a capstone and surface treatment like concrete, you expect to triple the cost.

5 rock

Construction of raised rock beds is an easy diy project for the average homeowner. Small boulders or large cobbles may be used and do not need to be mortared in place, provided that your wall is relatively low (12 inches or less, quite a reasonable height for raised beds). The beds can be straight or curved, as seen here, and the larger rocks can simply be pressed up against each other, while the smaller ones can be nestled together to create a boundary.

Pros: rock can produce a casual, cottage feel, and for most homeowners, it's a simple diy project. No special equipment is needed for this type of construction, and materials are readily available.

Cons: stacked or nestled rocks do not fit in any kind of landscape style. This form of design is not permanent, but it can also be considered an advantage if you want to alter the shape or position of your beds.

Cost: if you've already got rocks on your house, they're safe. When you don't, expect to pay $85 a cubic yard and up. Pop is priced by a cubic yard, pound or ton, so ask if the price is calculated for the type of rock you'd like to use before you buy it.

Landscape contractors will do this job with ease.

6.galvanized culvert

Galvanized culverts are usually used for highway drainage, but when to split into pieces, they will create beautifully stylish garden planters. Many building supplies stores sell ducts, but you can also search online for "free pick-up" ducts that are being disposed of.

Pros: culverts have a fresh contemporary look, are readily available, are easy to install (no assembly required) and can be a permanent feature in your garden. Also, you would have more control over the height and overall size of your planter than you would have if you were using stock tanks. Cons: you might have to call around to locate precisely what you want, and when you find a length of pipe in the desired width, you will need to pay to have it cut into sections to use as planters. To transport the parts home, you will need a truck, or you will have to arrange for delivery, usually at an additional cost. Culverts are more expensive than galvanized stock tanks.

Cost: culverts typically come in 20- to 30-foot lengths and a wide variety of widths. You could get 15 2-foot-tall, 36-inch-wide planters for about $900.

7.stock

 Tanks it can be one of the best choices for raised garden beds. Stock tanks, usually circular or rectangular with rounded ends, are commonly used to feed farm animals but have gained popularity in recent years as a great way to add urban chic to the garden. The only real work you'll have to do is install some drainage holes to the bottom of the tank, which can be quickly done with a 1⁄4-inch or 1⁄2-inch drill bit.

Pros: stock tanks are readily available in feed stores and are relatively inexpensive. There is no assembly required, and it will last indefinitely. They're also movable, which is useful if you redesign your garden layout. They're coming in a range of sizes. Cons: you're going to have to have a truck to carry stock tanks home or plan for delivery at an additional cost. The sides of the containers can heat up during the summer, but it's not typically a scorching heat that burns the skin.

Cost: stock tanks typically range from $30 to $150, depending on the size.

8.steel

Industrial elements like steel add a touch of rustic sophistication to any landscape. Iron, or more specifically cor-ten, is widely used in landscaping and construction projects and comes in 3/16 "or 1⁄4" thick sheets. When it is finished, the natural steel colour starts, and when the weather is perfect for a spectacular rusty patina. There are chemical processes that can quickly create a rusty patina, but care must be taken when applying it to prevent rusty runoff in nearby plantings or patios.

Pros: steel is a newer commodity in today's gardens, providing a stylish aesthetic. It also provides a slim profile where you want to identify beds but with a less bulky perimeter. It is inherently weather-resistant, making it a long-term addition.

Cons: this sort of raised bed is better left to the pros, as it can be challenging to build, and the material is heavy. It's a lot more costly and might not be available in all regions. It is also not recommended for areas that receive salt spray from the ocean, as the material may deteriorate rapidly. Steel may add to the heat of your soil, so it may not be the best option for heat-sensitive plants. The article itself can heat up faster than other raised bed materials, so i've found it beneficial to position it in a partially shaded area or to use plants that don't run over the hot edges.

Cost: a basic cor-ten rectangular planter box (2 by 6 feet) could sell for $1,200 or more depending on where you live.

Chapter Nine
The Best Soil Combination For Raised Garden Boxes

After you've built your beautiful raised garden boxes with the right materials, it's time to fill them up! The aim should be to make an environment for plants that is well aerated but retains moisture and nutrients, feeds roots, encourages worms and other microbial activity, and is essentially a living, breathing soil.

If you fill your raised garden boxes correctly, i assure you, your plants will flourish every time.

The best combination of land for raised garden beds should have two parts:

1. It's a strong base or rising medium.

2. High-quality improvements to feed the plants.

Part one growing medium

The compost is created when someone takes organic raw material and adds water and air. Over time, the bacteria break it down into an organic matter that doesn't look like the original materials they put in. Compost aims to provide the perfect environment for microbial production.

• you can get animal-based compost, which is chicken, donkey, pig, horse, or cow manure, which has fallen to the point that you can't say it's faeces any longer.

(names for animal-based compost: aged manure, composted manure, etc.) Or • you can get plant-based compost, which is wood chips, grass clippings, straw, leaves, kitchen scraps (and often eggshells).

(names for plant-based manure: manure, organic composted stuff, potting soil – has many ingredients as well, but most of them are composted.) Both work beautiful as a growing medium. You should never grow in compost alone, but it should be at least 30-50 per cent of your garden soil, whether you are making your soil in elevated garden boxes or applying it to your current soil for in-ground planting.

Coconut coir is a natural fibre made from the coconut husk. It is fully organic, as opposed to the widely used peat moss or sphagnum moss, which takes thousands of years to grow again. Coconut coir aims to keep the soil aerated while maintaining moisture and nutrients. Coconut coir also has a neutral ph and is more acidic than peat or sphagnum. (the only exception when i use peat or sphagnum is when i grow plants that require an acidic environment, such as strawberries or blueberries)

Part two | the plant food

 Making these changes will ensure that your plants have enough of food to develop into nutrient-rich plants.

• **worm castings** – where to purchase (1 bag per 3×8 raised garden box) – worm castings are worm poops. Oh boy, though, does that worm poop bring gold to your garden! It is such a perfect soil enricher and food for your plants as it not only provides a good source of nitrogen; it also attracts more worms to your garden. Parasites: an edible garden.

• **azomite** – where to buy (2 lb. For every 3×8 raised garden box) – azomite is rock dust. This has a lot of minerals and trace elements that you like back in your yard. Mineral degradation is a severe problem in our soil today. Apply it to your land, and your garden will thank you for generating high yields!

• **mycorrhizal fungi** – where to buy (1/2 cup per 3×8 raised garden box) – mycorrhizal fungi is a fungus that already exists in the soil. Still, it is crucial to add because it plays a vital role in producing a network of fungi that feeds the roots of your plants.

• **fish emulsion water** – where to buy (1/2 cup + 5-gallon bucket of water for the first watering) – it is optional, but i want to add one more thing to my soul, and that is a bucket full of fish emulsion water. Fish emulsion is an overall nutrient booster that supplies nitrogen, phosphorus and potassium along with trace elements.

Chapter Ten

Proven Tips To Help You Grow Vegetable, Herbs, And Flowers In Your New Raised Bed

7 high-yield vegetable garden tips

Even when you're tight on space imagine growing almost half a ton of delicious, gorgeous vegetables from a 15-to 20-foot plot, 100 pounds of tomatoes from just 100 square feet, or 20 pounds of carrots from only 24 square feet. Yields like this are more comfortable to achieve than you would expect. The key to super-productive gardening is that it takes time to prepare techniques that will work for your garden.

Below are seven high-yield techniques gleaned from

gardeners who have learned how to make the most of their garden space.

1. Plant in raised beds of fertile soil.

Expert gardeners believe that soil building is the single most significant element in driving up yields. Firm, organically fertile soil promotes the growth of healthy, extensive roots capable of accessing more nutrients and water. The result: extra-lush, extra-productive development above ground level.

The best way to get the deep layer of fertile soil is to set up beds. Growing beds yield up to four times more than the same amount of space planted in rows. This is due not only to their loose, fertile soil but also to their sufficient spacing. In using less space for pathways, you have more room to grow plants.

Raised beds will save you money, too. One researcher monitored the time it took to plant and maintain a 30-by-30-foot garden planted in beds and found that he had to spend just 27 hours in the garden between mid-may and mid-october. And he was able to collect 1,900 pounds of fresh vegetables. It is a year's supply of food for three people out of a minimum of three working days!

Why are the elevated beds saving so much time? Plants grow close enough to crowd out competing weeds, so you spend less time weeding. Close spacing also makes irrigation and harvesting more effective.

2. Round the soil out of your beds.

The shape of your beds can make a difference, too. Rising beds are more space-efficient by gently rounding the soil to form an arc. A rounded bed that is 5 feet long across its base, for example, might give you a 6-foot-wide above it. Maybe that food doesn't seem like much but multiplies it by the length of your garden, and you'll see that it can make a massive difference in the entire planting region.

For example, in a 20-foot-long field, mounding the soil in the middle increases your total planting area from 100 to 120 square feet. That's a 20% rise in planting space in a bed that takes up the same amount of field space. Lettuce, spinach and other greens are the ideal crops to grow on the edges of a rounded garden.

3. Plant the crop in triangles instead of rows.

Pay attention to how you arrange your plants to get the best yields from each bed. Do not plant in square patterns or rows. Instead, spread the plants by planting them in triangles. You can fit 10 to 14 per cent more plants in each bed by doing so.

Just be careful not to position your plants too firmly. Some plants do not hit their maximum size—or yield—when crowded. For example, when one researcher increased the distance between roman lettuces from 8 to 10 inches, the harvest weight of each plant doubled. (remember that weight yield per square foot is more important than the number of plants per square foot.) Overly close spacing can also stress plants, making them more vulnerable to disease and insect attack.

4. To capitalize on space, grow climbing plants.

No matter how small your garden is, you will produce more by going vertically. Grow space-hungry vineyard crops—such as tomatoes, pomegranates, peas, cabbage, melons, cukes, and so on—straight-up, protected by trellises, walls, cages, or stakes.

Growing vegetables vertically, too, saves time. Harvest and repairs are moving quicker since you can see precisely where the fruit is. Fungal diseases are also less likely to damage upward-bound plants due to increased air circulation around the foliage.

Consider growing vineyards on trellises on one side of raised beds, use sturdy end posts with nylon mesh net or chain in between to provide a climbing surface. Attach the growing vines to the grille. Yet don't worry about having firm fruits. Also, squash and melons can grow thicker support stems.

5. Choose compatible pairings.

Interplanting compatible crops also saves space. Consider the traditional native american mix of "three sisters": maize, beans and squash. Robust corn stalks support pole beans, while squash grows freely on the ground below, shading out competing weeds.

Many suitable combinations include tomatoes, basil and onions; leaf lettuce and peas or brass; carrots, onions and radishes; and beets and celery.

6. Time the crops very carefully.

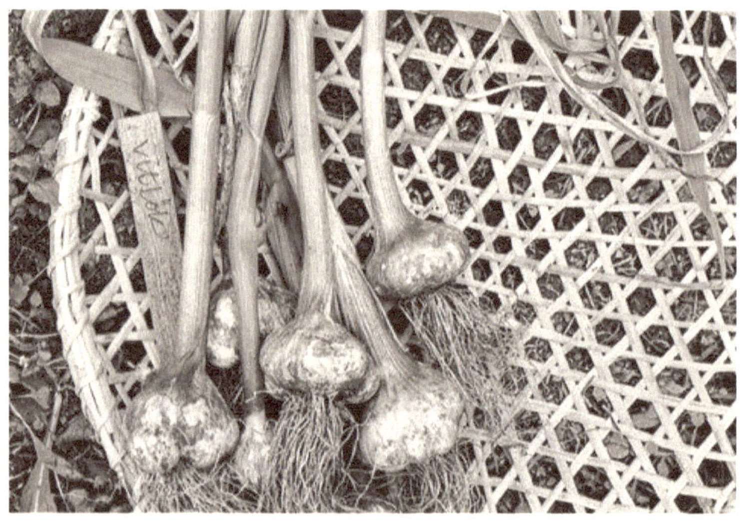

Succession planting helps you to grow more than one crop in a given area during the growing season. As a result, many gardeners can harvest three or even four crops from a single field. For example, following early leaf lettuce with fast-growing corn, and then develop more greens or overwintered garlic — all in a single growing season. • using transplants to get the most out of your succession plantings. The crop is a month or so old when you plant it, so it matures much faster than the seed sown directly in the garden.

• **select fast-growing varieties.**

• **replenish the soil with a 1⁄4 to 1⁄2** inch compost layer (about two cubic feet per 100 square feet) each time you replant. Work it in the top few inches of the soil.

7. Stretch your season by covering your sheets.

Adding a few weeks at each end of the growing season, you can buy enough time to grow another seed crop — say, leaf lettuce, kale, or turnip — or to pick more tomatoes at the end of the season.

You need to keep the air around your plants warm (even when the weather is cold) by using mulches, bells, row covers, or cold frames to get those extra weeks of growth.

Or give heat-loving crops (such as melons, peppers, and eggplants) an extra early start in the spring by using two "blankets "— one to warm the air and one to warm the soil. Approximately six to eight weeks before the last frost date, preheat cold ground by covering it with either infrared-transmitting (irt) mulch or black plastic that absorbs heat.

Then cover the bed with a small, transparent plastic tube once the soil temperature reaches 65 to 70 degrees fahrenheit, plant and wraps the black plastic mulch with straw to prevent it from trapping too much heat. Remove the transparent plastic tunnel when the temperature of the air warms, and the danger of frost has passed. Enable it again at the end of the season, when the temperatures are high.

Five quick steps to grow fresh herbs at home step 1: pick some pots

One of the main benefits of a home-grown herb garden is that it's always ready for action. Will you need to spice up the pasta or chicken roast? Only take a few leaves of basil, sage or thyme. With a bowl, you can put your herbs in convenient locations, such as on your porch, deck or kitchen counter.

The material in your container can vary. All choices are clay, wood, resin and metal. The most important thing is that it offers adequate drainage. Any pot or planter you use will allow excess water to escape, which is why most container bottoms have holes in them.

Mason jars are sweet to look at, but they don't make the best herb gardens out there. Without proper drainage, the herbs can inevitably undergo root rot.

Choose a container that fits the size of the herbs you cultivate. Choose anything too high, and your plants will spend too much energy developing their roots. A crowded planter allows the herbs to become root-bound (in other words, pot-bound). They're going to obstruct their nutrition, stress them or even injure them.

Phase 2: choose your herbs

If this is the first time you've tried growing herbs, it's simple to start. Parsley, mint and basil are an excellent way to create plants. They all seem to grow prolifically and don't mind regular harvesting. Below are some examples of the herbal varieties and their characteristics.

Basil

It is relatively easy to grow; basil prefers sunny locations. It also functions best in the fertile, well-watered soil.

Mint

With a rapid growth rate, mint is best put in its container and above ground. It can withstand shadow, but it is best suited to direct sunshine.

Oregan (greek)

This herb has thin, spicy leaves. It needs full sunshine and a lot of drainages. Greek oregano is also a perennial tender that you will have to put in during the winter months.

Parsley (flat-leaved)

Chefs prefer flat-leaved parsley over curly because it has more flavour. Parsley is ideally suited to moist, well-drained soils and can thrive in partially shaded areas.

Thyme this herb has very scented leaves and needs less water. You do need to give thyme maximum sunlight and well-drained soil exposure.

Rosemary

 The resinous rosemary leaves are strongly aromatic. The herb needs cold climates with plenty of sunlight and moist (not wet) soil. It's always safe to add rosemary to the winter indoors.

Phase 3: forget the seeds, use the starter plants

If you are an accomplished gardener, use the starter plants for your herbs. It will save you two to three weeks of growing time and increase your chances of a good harvest.

Phase 4: use the correct soil

When it's time to plant, use the potting soil — not the garden soil. Potting soil absorbs water more effectively. The former is lighter and translucent, while the latter is more substantial and traps (or blocks) moisture within the bottle. If you don't have one, pick up a spade from the yard. They're good at digging holes, handling soil, and removing weeds when needed.

Phase 5: care and harvesting

It requires continuous, daily treatment for herbs to grow. Which means you have to water them on a regular schedule. You're going to have to harvest them often, too, because this puts them at the forefront of new production. Only make sure you fit every treatment of your herbs to their particular range.

Get yours for today!

Starting a flower garden

If you've always dreamed of having a beautiful flower garden, now is the time to make it happen. Starting a flower garden is enjoyable and satisfying. Follow these instructions for beginners, and you're going to be off to a great start.

Step 1-know your garden • know your site: the first step in designing a perfect flower garden is to get acquainted with the place you want to plant. Landscape architect mary ellen cowan says, "you know your place. Listen to mother nature to learn about the characteristics of your land. Be realistic with sun, moisture and topography. "• know your soil: an important tip to ensure a good flower garden is to conduct a soil check. Erin benzakein, the owner of floret flower farm, says, "to obtain soil samples, dig a hole 1 foot deep, obtain a few teaspoons, and then repeat all over your garden until a quart-size container is complete. You can send your soil to a test lab like the umass soil and plant nutrient testing laboratory (soiltest.umass.edu) and use the tests to change your soil before planting. "• know your flowers: cowan also says," learn what plants grow best in your soil. From there, you can find out what to do with design-wise." carol bornstein, a horticulturist at the santa barbara botanic garden, suggests "visiting nearby natural areas that mimic your wild conditions to discover the flowers that you want." not sure where to start? Check out the following list:

The most natural flowers for beginners.

1. Know your frost cycle:

To ensure that your freshly planted garden survives the seasons, you will need to know your area's expected last and first frost dates. Benzakein states that this will influence when you start the seeds and will encourage you to plant varieties that will grow in the autumn. Starting your seeds about 4 to 6 weeks before the expected last frost date will give your plants a start. Plants are going to fill up quickly and cut down on weeds. If you don't have a greenhouse to start your seeds in, a covered seed tray should work indoors under rising lights.

Step 2-create your color palette

• **create unity:** when selecting a colour scheme, bornstein recommends selecting one that "helps to unify the landscape." variations and various shades of the same hue may affect without being dominant.

• **build excitement:**

When sticking to a few similar shades can build a sense of unity, contrasting colours—the opposites on the colour wheel—build juxtaposition. The combination of blue and yellow, for example, is young, vibrant, and summery. "in a sunny place, warm shades like yellows, oranges, and reds make the most of the sunshine, particularly during 'golden hours,' when the sun rises or sets. However, hot colours may appear very flat on their own. Blues complement the yellows, producing harmony and vibrancy. Occasional splashes of warm orange and red add a little spice, "says keith wiley of wildside, his garden in devon, england.

• **build safe areas:**

 Wiley adds that it is best to exercise caution because too much variation may sound exhausted. "you can't have it all shouting at you in the backyard. Separate areas of vivid colour or high contrast of neutrals" says bill thomas of chanticler. Above all, landscape designer and author of heaven is a garden, jan johnsen promotes the use of colours that you love in your garden.

Step 3-plan like a pro

• **plan with the form**: when planning a flower garden, the world-famous dutch garden designer piet oudolf suggests that way is an excellent place to start. Perennials have a variety of simple shapes: spires, plumes, daisies, arrows, globes, umbels, and screens. Try to bring together different ways to see if they set each other off. Some combinations may be lively and fluid, while others may be in tension. Planting similar flower shapes together will strengthen your concept.

• **repetitive design:**

The repetition of the main shapes or colours gives a sense of calm and visual unity. Ideally, wiley advises, the plants that you repeat will have a long season, do not look untidy after flowering, and flourish under the conditions of the garden. Strategic flower repetition provides consistency when going from one part of the garden to another.

• **layer design**:

Matt james, in his book, how to plant a garden, says, "when planting, try to pull one layer into another subtly — and vice versa — to build a more natural look, rather than simply arrange the layers like a staircase." oudolf notes that you might "lose plants in the back," so it's necessary to make sure the sightlines remain to see the flowers at the back of the border.

• **combination design:**

"talk of plant combinations rather than individual plants," says sean hogan of cistus nursery near portland, oregon. Mixing plant heights, sizes, shades, scales and textures keeps the garden engaged in all seasons. Relaxed plantings can give you light, movement and a meadow-like look.

• **build with fragrance and movement**:

Dan hinkley, a plant hunter and author, has discovered what he loves most in his garden—perfume and movement. "these elements of a garden are not often sufficiently included in the design." he recommends taking advantage of natural breeze patterns to allow the scents of flowers to waft into your home or patio areas.